2-12

D1306589

The Right to Be
SAFE

Putting an End to Bullying Behavior

CRICKET MEEHAN, PH.D.

SEARCH INSTITUTE PRESS

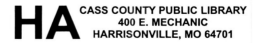

HA CASS COUNTY PUBLIC LIBRARY
400 E. MECHANIC
HARRISONVILLE, MO 64701

0 0022 0396282 0

The Right to Be Safe:
Putting an End to Bullying Behavior
Cricket Meehan, Ph.D.

Search Institute Press, Minneapolis, MN
Copyright © 2011 Search Institute

The following are registered trademarks of Search Institute: Search Institute®, Developmental Assets®, and Healthy Communities • Healthy Youth®.

All rights reserved. No parts of this publication may be reproduced in any manner, mechanical or electronic, without prior permission from the publisher except in brief quotations or summaries in articles or reviews, or as individual activity sheets for educational use only. For additional permission, write to Permissions at Search Institute.

At the time of publication, all facts and figures cited herein are the most current available; all telephone numbers, addresses, and website URLs are accurate and active; all publications, organizations, websites, and other resources exist as described in this book; and all efforts have been made to verify them. The author and Search Institute make no warranty or guarantee concerning the information and materials given out by organizations or content found at websites that are cited herein, and we are not responsible for any changes that occur after this book's publication. If you find an error or believe that a resource listed herein is not as described, please contact Client Services at Search Institute.

Printed on acid-free paper in the United States of America.

Search Institute
615 First Avenue Northeast, Suite 125
Minneapolis, MN 55413
www.search-institute.org
612-376-8955 • 877-240-7251, ext. 1

ISBN-13: 978-1-57482-491-9

Credits
Editor: Kate Brielmaier
Book Design: Percolator
Production Supervisor: Mary Ellen Buscher

Library of Congress Cataloging-in-Publication Data
Meehan, Cricket.
The right to be safe : putting an end to bullying behavior / by Cricket Meehan.
    p. cm.
  Includes bibliographical references and index.
  ISBN-13: 978-1-57482-491-9 (pbk. : alk. paper)
  ISBN-10: 1-57482-491-0 (pbk. : alk. paper)
  Bullying in schools—Prevention. 2. School violence—Prevention. 3. School children—Conduct of life. I. Title.
LB3013.3.M42 2011
371.7'82—dc22   2011006077

About Search Institute Press

Search Institute Press is a division of Search Institute, a nonprofit organization that provides catalytic leadership, breakthrough knowledge, and innovative resources to advance the health of children, youth, families, and communities. Our mission at Search Institute Press is to provide practical and hope-filled resources to help create a world in which all young people thrive. Our products are embedded in research, and the 40 Developmental Assets®—qualities, experiences, and relationships youth need to succeed—are a central focus of our resources. Our logo, the SIP flower, is a symbol of the thriving and healthy growth young people experience when they have an abundance of assets in their lives.

Licensing and Copyright

The educational activity sheets in *The Right to Be Safe: Putting an End to Bullying Behavior* may be copied as needed. For each copy, please respect the following guidelines:

• Do not remove, alter, or obscure the Search Institute credit and copyright information on any activity sheet.

• Clearly differentiate any material you add for local distribution from material prepared by Search Institute.

• Do not alter the Search Institute material in content or meaning.

• Do not resell the activity sheets for profit.

• Include the following attribution when you use the information from the activity sheets in other formats for promotional or educational purposes: **Reprinted with permission from *The Right to Be Safe: Putting an End to Bullying Behavior* by Cricket Meehan, Ph.D. [specify the title of the activity sheet you are quoting]. Copyright © 2011 Search Institute®, Minneapolis, MN; 877-240-7251 ext. 1; www.search-institute.org. All rights reserved.**

CONTENTS

ACKNOWLEDGMENTS

I would like to give a very special thank-you to Deb Robison, who saw Search Institute's "Call for Authors" for this book and thought of me. I appreciate your vote of confidence in my abilities to communicate with teachers and school professionals about such an important topic.

In addition, I would like to give a heartfelt thanks to Siri Bendtsen, Susan DeHart, Glenna Edwards, Sandy Smoot, Pam Turner, and Amy Wilms for taking time out of your busy schedules to read and review my chapters. Your feedback was invaluable! Thank you to Betsy Barringer, Siri Bendtsen, Betsy Cabell, and Karen Paul for providing me with resources and case studies. Special thanks to all my colleagues, especially the Olweus training directors at Clemson University, who are working to reduce and prevent violence in our schools and ensure that our children have the best opportunities to learn and to be successful in life, and to Stan Davis and CAPT Stephanie Bryn, who shared their tremendous insights about bullying behavior that they have gleaned from many years of working in this field. I have learned so much from you and much of that is reflected in this book.

Without the support of my editor, Kate Brielmaier, and her team at Search Institute, this book would not have been possible. Kate and her team recognized the importance of bringing concrete, tangible, and specific anti-bullying resources, tools, and strategies to teachers and school staffs. Thank you for supporting such a timely and pervasive concern in our society.

And finally, my deepest thanks to my husband, Michael Patrick, who provided me with unending love and support through the difficult task of writing this book in such a short period of time, and my son, Matthew David, who always made me laugh and motivated me to keep going.

INTRODUCTION

Historically, teachers have been tasked with the role of teaching students the three Rs: reading, writing, and arithmetic. Ensuring that students learned these basic academic skills constituted the breadth and scope of teacher-student relationships within the classroom setting. More recently, however, teachers are being asked (by governmental entities, legal organizations, educational institutions, and parents) to take on many additional roles within the classroom setting. For example, teachers oftentimes are expected to effectively discipline students exhibiting problematic behavior; build students' character, self-esteem, and self-confidence levels; develop positive values among students; provide counseling to students at risk of mental health problems; provide health and wellness advice to students at risk of health problems; serve as surrogate parents for students whose parents are unavailable; and be positive role models for their students, all while maintaining a strict adherence to teaching the academic content standards required by their educational authority

One thing remains overwhelmingly clear: teachers are expected to be masters of much more than simply teaching academic content to their students. Unfortunately, it is beyond the scope of this book to address every nonacademic barrier holding students back from being successful at school. Dating violence, involvement with gangs, substance use and abuse, antisocial behaviors, and criminal activity, among other problems, can be significant concerns for young people today. Teachers who have students facing these issues are encouraged to seek out professional development training opportunities to facilitate their ability to effectively teach students who face significant barriers to learning.

As it has become evident that teachers are required to address nonacademic barriers to learning, bullying behavior has risen as one of the most pervasive and challenging issues affecting students' abilities to be successful. Despite the expectation that teachers intervene to stop bullying behavior, few teacher-preparation programs provide teachers with the knowledge and know-how to effectively prevent and/or reduce bullying behaviors in their classrooms. This book was written to address many of the frequently asked questions that teachers have when facing bullying behaviors in their classrooms and schools. It is meant to be a comprehensive and educational guide to help teachers stop bullying behavior among students.

About This Book

Chapter 1 provides teachers with a complete look at bullying, including an examination of the definition and key components that make up bullying behavior. By helping teachers understand that bullying behavior is a form of peer abuse that significantly affects all students, teachers are better prepared to put a stop to abusive behavior. This book was written with a special emphasis on bullying as a *behavior* rather than an inherent characteristic of a student, and for that reason teachers are encouraged not to refer to students as *bullies* (or *victims*), instead emphasizing the behavior that students are engaging in. The primary focus of this book is on student safety and the role that teachers can play in keeping students safe through effective behavior management strategies.

Typically, students fall into one of three categories of bullying behavior: students who are being bullied, students who are bullying others, and students who are bystanders (or witnesses) to bullying. This book provides teachers with valuable information they can use to positively engage students. Chapters 2 and 3 identify the warning signs and indicators that bullying may be occurring and provide effective and evidence-based interventions for putting a stop to the abuse. Chapter 4 outlines the role that bystanders play in bullying, especially how their behavior reinforces or diminishes the likelihood of future bullying behavior. Bystanders say that one of the biggest barriers to helping students who are bullied is that they do not know how to help. This chapter presents specific and tangible strategies that teachers can use to help their students develop positive skills to support students who are being bullied.

In addition to supporting students in their anti-bullying efforts, this book outlines the role that caring, supportive teachers can take in reducing and/or preventing bullying. Chapter 5 outlines specific teacher-student relationship-building techniques that can not only enhance students' social, emotional, and behavioral well-being but also positively affect their academic success. Teachers can also foster a positive classroom culture and climate, and chapter 6 provides specific examples of tools that can assist in these efforts, such as classroom seating arrangements and decorations, rules and expectations for teacher-student interactions, and daily rituals and procedures.

Parents and guardians are critical partners in ensuring that students remain safe from harm, and chapter 7 highlights ways that teachers can collaborate with them to stop bullying behavior. This chapter highlights many of the reasons why parents/guardians do not engage school officials when they become aware of their child's involvement in bullying. It is important to understand and be respectful of everyone's perspective, and this chapter provides helpful guidance in navigating the process of partnering and collaborating with parents/guardians to keep their children safe from harm.

The remainder of the book consists of valuable resources. Chapter 8 provides guidance on creating school anti-bullying policies and procedures. The appendixes provide a historical look at the definition of bullying, information about evidence-based anti-bullying programs, legal information regarding bullying, and tools for finding funding for bullying prevention and intervention efforts. The practical and useful resources section contains examples of books, workbooks, websites and online resources, public service announcements, anti-bullying campaigns, videos, electronic resources, and tool kits that teachers may find useful for classroom or schoolwide anti-bullying efforts.

Taken together, the information provided in this book should be helpful to teachers who wish to address the complex and multifaceted nature of bullying behavior in schools today. The focus on bullying as a behavior is deliberate, and teachers are encouraged to shift their conceptualization of bullying accordingly. By taking this approach, we empower others to alter their behavior while recognizing the potential each person has to be the most positive, prosocial, caring, and supportive individual he or she can be.

CHAPTER 1

What Is Bullying and Why Should We Care?

Bullying is an underestimated and pervasive problem.
—GERARD KENNEDY, MINISTER OF EDUCATION, ONTARIO

The word *bullying* stirs emotions and evokes memories in most people. Shaped by these emotions and memories, an individual's personal experience is the single most important predictor of what he or she believes bullying is and what it looks like. Someone who has experienced bullying firsthand may describe the internal pain, trauma, and torment related to his or her own experience of bullying, but most people typically describe someone else's bullying experiences in visible, physical ways. For this reason, the general public's description of bullying usually includes some form of picking on or physically assaulting another person. While physical acts such as shoving, hitting, pushing, and kicking can be devastating and have significant consequences, it is crucial to understand all the different forms that bullying behavior may take, both visible and hidden.

BULLYING DEFINED

The definition of bullying has changed and evolved since researchers first started studying the phenomenon over 40 years ago (for a more complete look at the evolution of the definition of bullying, including a time line, please refer to appendix A). It has grown from simple descriptions of physical group violence against an individual to a more complex and nuanced explanation that takes into account power structures, verbal and indirect aggression, and changes over time, leading to this definition from Dan Olweus, a prominent bullying researcher:

> *A person is bullied when he or she is exposed, repeatedly and over time, to negative actions on the part of one or more other persons, and he or she has difficulty defending himself or herself.*

Olweus's definition is arguably the most widely accepted and used definition of bullying throughout the world, and it captures precise and distinct components of bullying behavior (discussed in more detail in the following section). Throughout this book, we will use this definition as the foundation of our discussions about bullying behavior.

COMPONENTS OF BULLYING

Three Key Components of Bullying

By understanding its unique characteristics, we are better able to accurately recognize and identify bullying behavior. Olweus's definition of bullying consists of three key components that will help us understand what bullying is and what it looks like:

1. Hurtful and purposeful aggressive behavior

2. Behavior that typically occurs repeatedly over a period of time

3. Behavior in which there is an imbalance of power and control between the parties involved[1]

   1. Hurtful, Purposeful Aggressive Behavior: Bullying behavior is meant to harm someone else. This type of behavior is not accidental in nature. Rather, the motivations behind bullying behavior are to be mean, cruel, and malicious to others. Children who engage in bullying behavior understand that what they are doing is unkind, but they make the purposeful choice to continue acting in a way that hurts other people.

   2. Repetitive in Nature: One of the primary reasons that students choose to continually harm others is that they receive some form of reinforcement for their behavior. Typically, this reinforcement comes from the bystanders who witness the event or from the students who are targeted. For example, students who witness the bullying behavior may laugh, cheer, or otherwise encourage the behavior to continue. Sometimes witnesses to bullying do this because they enjoy watching someone else being bullied. Other times, they reinforce the bullying behavior out of fear of being bullied themselves. They may believe that

F.A.Q.

Teachers and school staff often wonder, "Do I have to be sure that I know it is someone's intention to harm before I step in and intervene?" Although it can be difficult to know exactly what another person's intentions are, this is not an excuse to idly stand back and allow aggressive and harmful behavior to continue. Stopping abusive or otherwise harmful behavior is more important than investigating the specifics of the event. Once the student who is being harmed is safe, appropriate investigations can take place. Please refer to chapter 2 for more information about effectively intervening in bullying situations.

if they go along with the abuse they will not be singled out. Students who are targeted can also reinforce the bullying behavior by reacting in a way that is satisfying to the students engaging in the behavior (for example, by crying, begging for mercy, or following adults' advice to stand up to students who bully them). The students who bully may feel a sense of powerfulness or an ability to control the reactions of the students they target. The reinforcement that students who bully receive increases the likelihood that they will continue to act in the same way in the future.

3. *Imbalance of Power and Control:* Students who engage in bullying behavior typically choose the students they target carefully. They may select someone who is physically weaker, less athletic, less intelligent, less popular, less connected, or otherwise perceived as different from their peers. This creates an imbalance of power and control between the students (in favor of the student who bullies). The students who are targeted cannot defend themselves against a stronger, more athletic, smarter, and/or more popular peer. This inequity of power and control is the central reason why bullying is considered a form of peer abuse (see the "Bullying Is Peer Abuse" section below for more information).

Bullying Is a Behavior

Throughout this book, students who engage in bullying behavior will not be referred to as *bullies* or *perpetrators* and students who experience bullying will not be referred to as *victims* or *targets*. Rather, the act of bullying will be described as a *behavior* and not a permanent characteristic or trait of a student. This is an important distinction for the following reasons:

- By understanding that bullying is a behavior, we have the opportunity to use behavior management techniques (that is, positive reinforcement, negative reinforcement, punishment, and extinction) to alter undesirable behavior and replace it with more positive, prosocial behavior.

- By viewing someone's status as a victim, we imply that there is something inherent about that individual that makes her a natural target for individuals who bully others. Oftentimes, the only characteristic that distinguishes a student who is bullied from a student engaging in the bullying is that the student who is bullied is perceived as different in some way. For this reason, any one of us could become the target of someone who is stronger, more athletic, smarter, wealthier, more skilled at humor, better looking, or more popular than we (and who chooses to abuse this power).

- By viewing bullying as a permanent characteristic of the bully, we become hopeless and helpless to change the course of events.

 F.A.Q.

Teachers and school staff often ask, "Is it bullying if it happens only one time?" Certainly a single instance of purposeful, aggressive, and hurtful behavior toward someone who is unable to defend himself *is* bullying behavior and should be taken as seriously as multiple episodes of bullying. If the student who bullies receives reinforcement for that behavior, he is likely to repeat it in the future. Similarly, the inequity of power and control between the two parties will continue to exist unless something changes, making it very likely that the student will be targeted again.

If we believe that bullies will always bully and victims will always be targeted, there will be no use for a book of this nature. Fortunately, we know that bullying is a behavior that can be altered.

Bullying Is Peer Abuse

Bullying is a form of peer abuse in which there is an inequity of power and control (much like domestic violence) between the students who are bullying and the students who are being bullied. Students who engage in bullying behavior are purposefully trying to harm students who do not have the same power and control in the situation. When successful, the students participating in bullying behavior may be viewed as powerful, popular, cool, and feared by fellow classmates.

The following are some of the reasons why people engage in abusive behavior:

1. They have learned it (for example, they may have been abused by their parents or witnessed a parent abusing someone else).

2. They may have a mental health issue or disorder (for example, problems with anger or impulse control, substance abuse issues, or narcissism).

3. They may have an empathy deficit (they may have suffered from brain damage or never developed empathy) and cannot relate to others' feelings and emotions.

4. They benefit (that is, they receive positive reinforcement of some kind) from engaging in the abuse.

THE WHAT AND WHERE OF BULLYING BEHAVIOR

Direct and Indirect Bullying

Bullying typically takes one of two forms: direct bullying or indirect bullying. Direct bullying is often described as physical bullying because it includes behaviors such as hitting, kicking, biting, pushing, shoving, spitting, teasing, taunting, name calling, threats, and obscene gestures. Oftentimes these are the behaviors that prompt disciplinary action because teachers and other adults in the school setting witness them occurring or can verify that they occurred because the student who was bullied has physical marks on his body following the abuse (like teeth marks, bruises, cuts, or lacerations).

Indirect bullying is often called relational bullying and is much more difficult to witness directly. It typically includes behaviors such as using relationships to bully others, spreading rumors, getting another

NOTE It is very important to understand the gravity of peer abuse. Most people can readily understand the harmful relationship dynamics that occur in cases of domestic violence and spousal abuse. Peer abuse (bullying) should also be thought of in this respect. In both cases, someone is using manipulative, aggressive, and hurtful behavior to gain power, control, and domination over someone else for personal gratification. Also, in both cases, the individual being abused is not responsible for the abuse and should not be expected to stop it. Too often in bullying situations, we blame the people being targeted for their situation and chastise them for not doing enough to get out of the situation. This, quite simply, is an unfair and dangerous attitude. People who are being abused need others' help to stop their abuse and should never be held responsible for the abuse.

person to bully someone, isolating someone socially from her peers, and cyberbullying. These behaviors can be much more difficult for adults at school to identify accurately, making it hard to intervene appropriately. As a result, indirect bullying may continue for extended periods of time without adults in the school being aware that it is going on.

Where Does Bullying Occur?

Bullying can occur in a wide variety of settings, both in school and outside the school setting and with or without adults present. Bullying researcher Catherine Bradshaw and her colleagues found that elementary students reported that bullying was most likely to occur on the playground, in the classroom, and in the cafeteria. Among middle and high school students, bullying most likely took place in the classroom, in the cafeteria, in the hallways, and at their lockers.[2]

PERCENTAGE OF STUDENTS REPORTING THE OCCURRENCE OF BULLYING IN DIFFERENT SCHOOL LOCATIONS

LOCATIONS	ELEMENTARY SCHOOL STUDENTS	JUNIOR HIGH/MIDDLE SCHOOL STUDENTS	HIGH SCHOOL STUDENTS
Classroom/Class	21%	29%	24%
Hallway/Lockers	15%	29%	21%
Cafeteria/Lunch	20%	23%	20%
Gym/PE	10%	20%	15%
Bathroom	5%	12%	13%
Playground/Recess	30%	6%	10%

The locations where bullying occurs can vary widely from one school to another. In general, locations that are closely monitored through good supervision and surveillance are less likely to promote bullying behaviors, while locations with less supervision and surveillance are more likely to promote the emergence of bullying behaviors. Every school and classroom is unique, and school locations should be reviewed to determine whether or not bullying is occurring there.

With the advent of technology, more and more bullying is happening in the cyber realm. This type of electronic aggression has been called cyberbullying, flaming, sexting, outing, and cyberstalking. It can occur anywhere that students have access to an electronic device (like a computer, a cell phone, or an Xbox), whether at home, at school, or in the community. In some cases, cyberbullying that occurs outside the school setting can have a substantial impact within the school setting. For a discussion about the legal responsibility that schools and

NOTE A common saying sums up what many adults believe to be the difference between direct and indirect bullying: "Sticks and stones may break my bones, but words will never hurt me." "Sticks and stones may break my bones" refers to harming someone in a physical manner and may refer to physical bullying behaviors. Assaulting another person (whether bullying or not) is clearly wrong and has serious consequences in our society. The second half of the saying, "words will never hurt me," demonstrates a myth held by many people that psychological abuse is not as harmful as physical abuse. This is simply not true. We know that indirect, relational bullying can and *does* hurt.

districts have toward bullying and cyberbullying that occurs off campus but that substantially affects the school environment, please refer to appendix C.

BEHAVIOR THAT IS NOT BULLYING

In order to understand what is and what is not bullying, it is important to identify behaviors that share some similarities with bullying but that are, in fact, something else. Bullying is considered a subset of aggressive behavior. Aggressive behavior, however, can include aggressive forms of communication in younger children, fighting among older children, physical assaults, aggression in mental health disorders (such as conduct disorder or oppositional defiant disorder), conflicts and disagreements, and aggressive play (that is, rough play and horseplay) among friends.

Aggression as Communication

Younger children who find it difficult to communicate using their words may resort to physically aggressive ways of communicating. They may bite or hit one of their peers when they become frustrated and unable to communicate in a more appropriate manner. Although this behavior is considered harmful and aggressive, it is not considered bullying behavior. In this circumstance, the imbalance of power is most likely reversed, with the student who has been kicked or bitten having more developed communication skills than the child engaging in the behavior. Children who are experiencing communication difficulties may benefit from speech and language therapy and services rather than disciplinary action for bullying their peers.

Aggression in Mental Health Disorders

Some children engage in aggressive behavior due to a mental health disorder. The defining characteristics of conduct disorder include aggressive behavior, destruction of property, deceitfulness, theft, and the serious violation of rules. While bullying behavior may be one of the problems a child with conduct disorder exhibits, there are typically many other types of problematic behaviors that, taken as a whole, lead to this more intense clinical diagnosis. The defining characteristics of oppositional defiant disorder include aggressive behavior toward authority figures, meaning the aggression is typically directed toward an adult such as a parent or teacher. In general, this would not be considered bullying as the adult is in a position of power in relation to the student, so the imbalance of power definition would not be met. Students

NOTE Distinguishing between different forms of aggressive behavior does not mean that adults have more or less of a responsibility to intervene to end the aggressive behavior depending on which type of aggression students are engaging in. Rather, it means that interventions that are most appropriate to the type of aggressive behavior being displayed will be most likely to be successful in ending the problematic behavior and should be taken into consideration whenever possible.

with mental health disorders should be referred to school-based or community-based mental health services. While their treatment may include strategies that are effective for reducing bullying (including consequences for breaking rules), this will likely occur in the context of a broader treatment plan addressing all their symptoms.

Aggression in Developmental Disabilities

Children who have severe developmental delays in their language and communication skills may also exhibit aggressive behavior, sometimes in a frustrated attempt to communicate. In some cases, their aggressive behavior may be a direct reaction to other students bullying them, since fellow classmates may tease children with severe developmental delays. In response, these children may struggle to communicate their unease, anxiety, and hurt at being teased and their actions may be hostile and aggressive. These children would benefit from speech and language therapy to improve their communication skills and reduce their levels of frustration at not being able to communicate with others effectively.

Rough Play among Friends

Friends often engage in rough play. While this may appear to be bullying, the students involved have no intention of harming one another; they are just showing their affection and friendship in an aggressive way. Regardless of intent, this behavior can be disruptive to the school environment, and there may need to be rules in place to prohibit rough play while at school. More important, adults should be aware that some students might claim that their behavior is just rough play with someone who is their friend when in reality they are engaging in bullying behavior with someone who is not their friend.

Conflicts and Disagreements

Conflicts and disagreements between two people or groups of people occur when both parties believe that their point of view is correct and they cannot accept the other party's point of view. Although conflicts can sometimes look like bullying, there is not usually an imbalance of power between the individuals in disagreement with one another. Conflict resolution and mediation strategies have sometimes been used interchangeably in true conflict scenarios and in bullying scenarios. The strategies assume equal power and control among the parties so a compromise or resolution can be made. In the case of conflicts and disagreements, conflict resolution strategies may be very effective, but they are not effective in bullying situations.

Fighting and Assaults

Purposeful, harmful behavior can also occur between students who are relatively equal peers. They may share similar physical strength, intelligence, social status, or other characteristics, but for whatever reason, they want to do each other harm. In most cases, this type of behavior is considered fighting or assaulting. Usually, fights and assaults occur because the individual feels wronged by the other person or party. In these cases, the school's disciplinary procedures prohibiting fighting should be followed. Conflict resolution and mediation strategies can be effective in many situations involving fighting and assaults. For severe situations, law enforcement officials may need to be involved.

COMPARING TYPES OF AGGRESSIVE BEHAVIOR WITH THE KEY COMPONENTS OF BULLYING BEHAVIOR

		Key Components of Bullying		
		HURTFUL, AGGRESSIVE BEHAVIOR	PURPOSEFUL, AGGRESSIVE BEHAVIOR	REPEATED BEHAVIOR (TYPICALLY)	IMBALANCE OF POWER AND CONTROL
Types of Aggressive Behavior	**BULLYING (DIRECT AND INDIRECT)**	Yes	Yes	Yes	Yes
	AGGRESSIVE COMMUNICATION	Yes (although typically out of frustration)	No	Sometimes	Reversed
	AGGRESSION IN MENTAL HEALTH DISORDERS	Sometimes	Sometimes	Sometimes	Reversed
	AGGRESSION IN DEVELOPMENTAL DISABILITIES	Yes (although typically out of frustration)	No	Sometimes	Reversed
	ROUGH PLAY/HORSEPLAY	Sometimes	Yes	Sometimes	No
	CONFLICTS AND DISAGREEMENTS	Yes	Yes	Sometimes	No
	FIGHTING/ASSAULTS	Yes	Yes	Yes	No

EFFECTS OF BULLYING

Researchers have uncovered many short- and long-term effects of bullying behavior on students. There are consequences not only for the students who are bullied and the students who bully but also for the students who witness bullying. The following sections describe the physical, psychological, social, emotional, behavioral, and academic effects of involvement in bullying behavior.

On Children Who Are Bullied

Overwhelmingly, students who are bullied are the focus of the majority of research examining the consequences of bullying. Researchers have identified many ways that children who are bullied are affected as a result of their abuse: physically, psychologically, socially, emotionally, behaviorally, and academically. The lists on the first side of the following handout outline the numerous challenges faced by students who are abused by their peers, with shorter-term consequences listed first and longer-term consequences listed later.

Chapter 2, "Students Who Are Bullied: Ways Teachers Can Help," provides more detailed information about how teachers can recognize the warning signs that students are being bullied and ways that they can intervene to stop the abuse.

On Children Who Bully

Researchers have identified three main ways that children who bully experience consequences as a result of their behavior.[3] These students face emotional, behavioral, and academic ramifications, with a primary emphasis on behavioral effects. The lists on the second page of the following handout outline the challenges faced by students who bully, with shorter-term consequences listed first and longer-term consequences listed later.

Chapter 3, "Students Who Bully: Ways to Change Behavior," provides more detailed information about risk factors that increase the likelihood that students will engage in bullying behavior, along with practical ways teachers can intervene to stop bullying.

On Children Who Witness Bullying

Although we often talk about the role that children who witness bullying play, very little research has been conducted to uncover the consequences these students face following their observation of (and perhaps participation in) bullying situations. In one of the only known studies to date, Ian Rivers and his colleagues identified psychological,

Short- and Long-Term Consequences of Being Bullied

Physical

- Injuries
- Bruises
- Scrapes
- Lacerations
- Black eyes
- Torn clothing
- Damaged property
- Missing property
- Physical ailments
- Broken bones
- Internal injuries

Psychological

- Psychiatric/psychological symptoms
- Stress
- Panic
- Impaired concentration
- Problems sleeping
- Nightmares
- Recurrent intrusive memories
- Poor self-esteem
- High rates of referral to psychological services
- Suicidal thoughts
- Suicide attempts/ completion

Social

- Apprehension
- Feelings of abandonment
- Insecurity
- Difficulty with relationships
- Difficulty making friends
- Poor social adjustment
- Social isolation
- Being less popular at school
- Poor peer relationships (few, if any, friends)
- Lack of trust and intimacy in relationships
- Difficulty (as an adult) with relationships

Emotional

- Poor emotional adjustment
- Unhappiness
- Sadness
- Irritability
- Nervousness
- Loneliness
- Feeling unsafe
- Fear
- Anxiety
- Depression
- Helplessness/ hopelessness

Behavioral

- Psychosomatic complaints (headaches, stomachaches)
- Uncooperative
- Hyperactivity
- Shyness
- Avoidance of certain places (restroom, hallways)
- Absenteeism
- Bringing weapons to school (for protection)
- Submissiveness
- Eating disorders
- Shyness (as an adult)
- Acts of retribution (homicide)

Academic

- Inability to focus on schoolwork
- Withdrawal from classes and school
- Lack of confidence in front of peers
- Poor academic performance
- Poor grades
- Poor academic achievement
- Lack of interest in school
- Quitting activities
- Skipping school
- Dropping out of school
- Giving up on one's future

Short- and Long-Term Consequences of Engaging in Bullying Behavior

Emotional

- Anxiety
- Lack of Empathy
- Depression

Behavioral

- Psychosomatic complaints
- Antisocial behavior
- Delinquent behavior
- Shoplifting
- Carrying weapons
- Drinking alcohol
- Using illicit drugs
- Traffic violations
  (as an adult)
- Criminal convictions
  (as an adult)
- Aggression toward spouse
  (as an adult)
- Use of severe punishment
  with one's children
  (as an adult)

Academic

- Dislikes school
- Disengagement from school
- Underachievement in school

This handout may be reproduced for educational, noncommercial uses only (with this copyright line). From *The Right to Be Safe: Putting an End to Bullying Behavior* by Cricket Meehan, Ph.D. Copyright © 2011 Search Institute®, Minneapolis, MN; 877-240-7251 ext. 1; www.search-institute.org. All rights reserved.

social, and behavioral consequences faced by children who witness bullying behavior. They found that students who witness bullying have higher levels of mental health problems, are more uncomfortable in interpersonal situations, and use more alcohol and drugs as a result of their experiences.[4]

Chapter 4, "The Role of Bystanders: How School and Classroom Climate Can Make a Difference," provides more detailed information about the role that students who witness bullying can play in increasing or diminishing bullying behavior, with an emphasis on specific tools and strategies that can boost their skills, abilities, and confidence levels to help others.

STUDENTS' SAFETY

How Prevalent Is Bullying?

Bullying prevalence rates can vary based on survey methods, but in one of the most widely cited studies, researcher Tonja Nansel and her colleagues discovered that 30 percent of middle and high school students (6th to 12th graders) were involved in bullying, either as students who were bullying (13 percent of students), students who were being bullied (11 percent of students), or students who were both bullying others and being bullied themselves (6 percent of students).[5] In a typical classroom of about 20 students, this means there will be approximately 3 students who abuse their peers, 2 students who are being abused, and 1 student who is both abusing others and being abused. Among the over 58 million students attending primary and secondary schools in the United States, this equates to more than 17.4 million students who are directly involved in bullying across the country. The remaining students in the classroom will likely be indirectly involved in bullying as bystanders or witnesses.

As alarming as these statistics are, more recent research conducted by Catherine Bradshaw and her colleagues shows even higher rates of bullying among a group of elementary, middle, and high school students. Bradshaw and her colleagues found that nearly half of students (49 percent) reported being bullied by others and nearly one-third of students (31 percent) reported bullying others.[6] This indicates that the overwhelming majority of students are directly involved in bullying. A study in which the Olweus Bullying Questionnaire was administered to over half a million 3rd- through 12th-grade students found that 17 percent of students reported being bullied and 10 percent of students reported bullying others.[7] Despite the discrepancy in these statistics, one thing is certain: bullying occurs regularly and often, and we must address this problematic behavior.

As a result of the impact that bullying has on nearly every student in the classroom, it is essential that teachers and other adults in the school building understand the different types of bullying (the what) and the different places (the where) that bullying can take place. Chapters 2, 3, and 4 discuss the who and why of bullying. As for the when, the short answer is that bullying can happen anytime.

According to the 2007 U.S. Census, over 58 million students attend primary and secondary schools in the United States. Based on the results from the national Olweus Bullying Questionnaire database of over 500,000 students in grades 3 through 12, one in six students (17 percent) reported being bullied on school property during the previous 12 months. This equates to 9.8 million students who are bullied every year at school. For every six students in a classroom, it is likely that one of them is experiencing some of the consequences of being bullied (listed in the previous section), making it difficult for him to achieve his academic potential. The remaining students in the classroom are likely witnessing (and being affected by) bullying. It is imperative that teachers and other adults intervene to keep these students safe in their classrooms and at school.

Chapter 5, "The Role of Teachers: The Impact of Positive, Caring Adults," provides specific and detailed relationship-building techniques that can foster a nurturing and supportive environment in which students' safety, academic potential, and personal well-being can be enhanced.

The Right to Be Safe at School

All students have the right to attend a school in which they feel safe. The Safe and Drug-Free Schools and Communities Act (SDFSCA) was signed into law on January 8, 2002.[8] SDFSCA has four overarching goals: (1) to prevent violence in schools, (2) to prevent illegal use of substances (that is, alcohol, tobacco, and illicit drugs), (3) to involve parents and community members, and (4) to create safe and drug-free learning environments that will help students achieve academically. In tandem with creating a drug-free school environment for students, SDFSCA works to prevent violent, aggressive behavior such as bullying at school.

Anti-Bullying Laws and Legislation

In addition to the federal SDFSCA, most states have adopted anti-bullying legislation. In the United States (as of May 2011), 46 states (see the map on page 128 in appendix C) have anti-bullying legislation in place according to Bully Police, a watchdog organization that advocates for children who are bullied (bullypolice.org). Please refer to appendix C, "U.S. Federal and State Laws Regarding Bullying: Implications for Schools," for a detailed discussion about anti-bullying laws and legislation in the United States.

PUTTING A FACE ON BULLYING

In order to better understand the phenomenon of bullying, it is helpful to read the stories of individuals who have been involved in different aspects of bullying. The following four stories describe bullying from four different perspectives: (1) the role of physical strength in bullying behavior, (2) the use of technology to attack someone, (3) the role disabilities play in bullying, and (4) the story of a child with major medical problems. While the names and identifying information have been changed in each of the stories, all are based on actual events.

"Best All-Around Boy"

Imagine living in a small community in the midwestern United States where everyone knows everyone else. Now imagine that you are an 8th-grade boy whose growth spurt has occurred sooner than any of your peers. You are nearly 6 feet tall, muscular, and athletic, and you have the early beginnings of a beard. Meet Trevor. This is his story.

Trevor, who has always been athletic, excels in all the sports in which he participates. He is an excellent student, a highly ranked Boy Scout, and a well-regarded trumpet player in his school band. Trevor is unusually engaging for a middle school boy and is well thought of by the teachers and staff at his middle school.

Despite the overall appearance of a well-rounded student, Trevor's friends and classmates know a different side of him. Shortly after his growth spurt, Trevor began to physically assault his smaller, less developed male classmates. These behaviors began as occasional punches to the arms of classmates passing by him between classes. Enjoying the reactions that he received from his classmates as a result of his attacks, Trevor increased his repetitive and aggressive behaviors. He often punched, slapped, and shoved male classmates during lunchtime. His inappropriate behavior soon moved into the classroom prior to the start of class while teachers were still monitoring the flow of traffic in the hallways. Hitting smaller boys in the groin or placing them into uncomfortable holds became a daily occurrence. When one student would physically or verbally defend himself, Trevor would find another student who would not. Trevor especially seemed to enjoy picking on one particular student who was involved in the school's theater productions and who gave the understandable but dramatic injured performance that Trevor was seeking.

NOTE Throughout the other chapters of this book, these case stories will be revisited so we can learn from them how to recognize and identify warning signs of bullying, teach appropriate ways to intervene in each type of situation, and partner with parents, community members, and others to ensure that our students are safe.

Students who witnessed this behavior kept silent for fear of receiving the abuse themselves. Trevor was clever enough to engage in his bullying behaviors in congested classrooms, hallways, and playgrounds when teachers were most likely to be distracted. In the meantime, he continued to be a model student, musician, athlete, and young citizen whenever adults were present. Having noticed his competitive drive, success in and out of the classroom, and disciplined ambition, the 8th-grade teachers and staff rewarded him by electing him "Best All-Around Boy" of that school year, unaware that he abused his peers.

Using Technology to Bully

Meet Jenny: a conscientious student, a second-chair violinist, a member of the pep club, and a varsity cheerleader at a large suburban high school in the southern United States. Jenny and three of her friends were considered very popular at school and enjoyed the exclusive and powerful role of setting the standard for what to wear, who was in and out, where to work, what to drive, and what to do with one's free time. Things seemed to be perfect for Jenny, until her friends became increasingly mean in their comments to other students. Uncomfortable being associated with their behavior, Jenny began to distance herself from her friends. She stopped participating in their teasing of others, stopped returning their calls, and began eating lunch with members of the school orchestra instead of with them. Unaccustomed to being rejected by anyone, the three girls accused Jenny of being a goody-goody and said she wasn't fun anymore. Their accusations and teasing made her want to spend even less time in their presence, and she began avoiding them outside of class and at cheering events.

Jenny's former friends began to repeatedly verbally harass and intimidate Jenny. One of them told Jenny she better watch her back while cheering. This caused Jenny, a "flyer" for the cheerleading team, to wonder if they would intentionally allow her to fall and be injured. Afraid of making things worse and believing that she was old enough to handle the situation by herself, especially because adults may have encouraged her not to tattle on others, Jenny did not report their continually increasing harassment to her coach or parents and minimized it when questioned by her peers. Her attempts to further ignore or exclude her former friends from her life only served to make them angrier and more aggressive.

One day in history class, Jenny asked to be excused to go to the bathroom. One of her former friends, who was also in her history class, thought up a plan to attack Jenny and used her cell phone to text the other two girls in two separate classes, telling them to meet Jenny in the third-floor bathroom. Each of the other two girls asked their respective teachers for a bathroom pass and surprised Jenny in the bathroom at the far end of the third-floor hallway. During the confrontation, they threatened her, pulled her hair, and shoved her head into one of the toilet bowls, leaving her bruised, sore, and wet. The two girls told Jenny that they would make her life miserable if she told anyone what had happened.

Jenny, afraid and embarrassed to return to class, drove home and skipped the remainder of her classes that day. The teachers and staff were unaware that anything had occurred until repeated absences from class and cheerleading practice led Jenny to confess to her parents what was taking place at school.

When Children Have Disabilities

Ethan is the unusual child in his 3rd-grade elementary school classroom. Diagnosed with Asperger syndrome and ADHD, Ethan often has unusual and lengthy conversations with his peers in which he explains the intricate complexities of Pokémon cards. Ethan rarely lets his classmates respond but rather talks at them. Throughout the day, he often gets out of his seat, walks to the cabinet in the back of the room, looks out the windows, and rearranges stacks of papers and supplies in the classroom. If the routine in the classroom changes, Ethan has a meltdown and is inconsolable. Ethan may also have some symptoms of Tourette syndrome as he occasionally lets out a shrill, ear-piercing screech.

Overall, the students in Ethan's classroom have learned to ignore his behavior in the classroom and move on with their own schoolwork. Unfortunately, though, the students began teasing Ethan about his peculiar behavior during recess. Ethan's parents contacted the school to discuss the matter and decided that Ethan's mother would come into the classroom to talk with the students in a frank and direct manner about Ethan's disabilities. Ethan also shared his thoughts and feelings about his disabilities with his classmates during the meeting. Following these discussions, the students appeared to have more empathy for Ethan and the teasing stopped. Additionally, Ethan's classmates became very protective of him when he was around students from other classes.

After Major Medical Procedures

When he was in middle school, Ben had five surgeries on his feet and legs due to a growth problem. Each surgery required that Ben not put any kind of pressure on his feet for 8 to 10 weeks, followed by six months of rehabilitation therapy. At the end of each recovery period, Ben started the process all over again for his consecutive surgeries, which lasted throughout his entire middle school experience. It was during this time that the bullying started.

During grades 6 and 7, Ben was the target of teasing and bullying. Unfortunately, though, Ben's bullying became quite frequent and severe during grade 8. During that year, Ben's classmates would try to push him out of his wheelchair, which he needed to get around school. Some of the students began calling him a cripple and some even wrote this in his yearbook.

Over the summer, Ben was hopeful that his move to high school, along with the fact that he no longer needed surgeries, would end the bullying. Unfortunately, it did not. During grade 9, Ben finally told his mother that he had to switch schools because he was being picked on and it was making his life miserable. Ben said the other students were mean to him and called him names, pushed him against the lockers when he walked by, laughed at him, and talked about him behind his back. Despite telling his mother what was happening, Ben would not tell her the names of the people who were targeting him because he did not want to be considered a snitch.

The day before finals, one of the boys who bullied Ben slapped him in the face in the hallway, and everyone watching laughed. Ben knew that if he fought back, he would be suspended from school and would receive zeros on all his finals. But because he chose not to fight back, the students began calling him even worse names.

Later that day, one of the popular boys in school sent Ben several text messages from home that were threatening and demoralizing and contained a lot of profanity. This student logged into his Xbox account and told all of Ben's classmates to delete Ben from their Xbox accounts. Every student, including many whom Ben considered friends, deleted him.

Notes

1. D. Olweus (1993), *Bullying at school: what we know and what we can do,* Cambridge, MA: Blackwell Publishers, Inc.; D. Olweus (1999), "Sweden," in P.K. Smith, Y. Morita, J. Junger-Tas, D. Olweus, R. Catalano, & P. Slee (Eds.), *The nature of school bullying: A cross-national perspective* (7–27). New York: Routledge.

2. C.P. Bradshaw, A.L. Sawyer, & L.M. O'Brennan, (2007). "Bullying and peer victimization at school: Perceptual differences between students and school staff." *School Psychology Review, 36*(3), 361–382.

3. O. Aluede (2006), "Bullying in schools: A form of child abuse in schools," *Educational Research Quarterly, 30*(1), 37–49; A.G. Carney & K.W. Merrell (2001), "Bullying in schools: Perspectives on understanding and preventing an international problem," *School Psychology International, 22,* 364–381; D. Farrington (1993), "Understanding and preventing bullying," in M. Tonry (Ed.), *Crime and justice: A review of research,* (Vol. 17, 381–458), Chicago: University of Chicago Press; R. Forero et al. (1999), "Bullying behavior and psychosocial health among school students in New South Wales, Australia: Cross-sectional survey," *BMJ, 319,* 344–348; G. M. Glew et al. (2005), "Bullying, psychosocial adjustment, and academic performance in elementary school," *Archives of*

Pediatric & Adolescent Medicine, 159, 1026–1031; D.L. Haynie et al. (2001), "Bullies, victims, and bully/victims: Distinct groups of at-risk youth," *Journal of Early Adolescence, 21,* 29–49; R. Kaltiala-Heino et al. (2000), "Bullying at school: An indicator of adolescents at risk for mental disorders," *Journal of Adolescence, 23,* 661–674; T. Nansel et al. (2001), "Bullying behaviors among US youth: Prevalence and association with psychosocial adjustment," *Journal of the American Medical Association, 285,* 2094–2100; D. Olweus (1995), "Bullying or peer abuse at school: Facts and intervention," *Current Directions in Psychological Science, 4*(6), 196–201; D. Olweus (1997), "Bully/victim problems in school: Facts and intervention," *European Journal of Psychology of Education, 12*(4), 495–510; W. Roberts (2000), "The bully as victim: Understanding bully behaviors to increase the effectiveness of interventions in the bully-victim dyad," *Professional School Counseling, 4*(2), 148–154; G. Salmon et al. (2000), "Bullying a review: Presentations to an adolescent psychiatric service and within a school for emotionally and behaviourally disturbed children," *Clinical Child Psychology and Psychiatry, 5*(4), 563–579; A. Sourander et al. (2006), "Childhood predictors of male criminality: A prospective population-based follow-up study from age eight to late adolescence," *Journal of the American Academy of Child and Adolescent Psychiatry, 45,* 578–586; M. F. Van der Wal et al. (2003), "Psychosocial health among young victims and offenders of direct and indirect bullying," *Pediatrics, 111*(6), 1312–1317.

4. I. Rivers, et al. (2009). "Observing bullying at school: The mental health implications of witness status." *School Psychology Quarterly, 24*(4), 211–223.

5. T. Nansel et al. (2001), "Bullying behaviors among US youth: Prevalence and association with psychosocial adjustment," *Journal of the American Medical Association, 285,* 2094–2100.

6. C.P. Bradshaw, A.L. Sawyer, & L.M. O'Brennan, (2007). "Bullying and peer victimization at school: Perceptual differences between students and school staff." *School Psychology Review, 36*(3), 361–382.

7. D. Olweus & S. Limber (October 20, 2010), "Bullying in the U.S.: Are we making the grade?" [Webinar].

8. Title IV, Part A of the Elementary and Secondary Education Act.

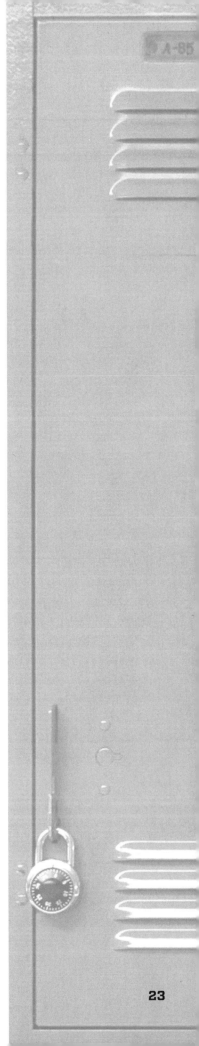

CHAPTER 2

Students Who Are Bullied: Ways Teachers Can Help

I just want them to stop. I can't take it anymore. I used to love coming to school, but now I hate it.

—VERITY WARD, PRIMARY SCHOOL STUDENT

Direct bullying includes behaviors such as hitting, kicking, biting, pushing, shoving, spitting, teasing, taunting, name calling, and making threats and obscene gestures. Indirect bullying includes behaviors such as relational bullying, spreading rumors, getting another person to bully someone, subjecting someone to social isolation, and cyberbullying. Once the behaviors have been accurately identified, appropriate intervention strategies to address those behaviors can be implemented.

WARNING SIGNS OF BEING BULLIED

Physical Indicators

Oftentimes there are visible signs that a student is being bullied. The student may have torn, damaged, or soiled clothing as a result of abusive peers pushing, shoving, kicking, or tripping her. It is especially important to note any changes that may occur during the school day (that is, clothing that was not torn earlier in the day but that has dirt stains or tears in it later in the day). Students who are frequently reporting missing or damaged items such as books or homework with no explanation (or an unlikely explanation) may be losing their possessions to others who are taking them as a form of bullying. Another physical indicator of bullying is the appearance of unexplained cuts, bruises, and scratches.

Adults at school should pay special attention to students who are being picked on or teased by other students. Some students who have been abused by their peers make the decision to bring some form of protection, such as a weapon, to school. Students who feel that they have no other way of stopping the abuse may resort to revenge or violence against the peers who hurt them.

Social Indicators

Students who experience bullying may be targeted because they are not as socially skilled as some of their peers. Many students who experience bullying have very few, if any, friends. They may be withdrawn and shy in social activities. These students tend to be socially isolated from the rest of the students in school. They may be hesitant to join social groups and activities for fear that they will be rejected and abused by their peers. Some students who are isolated turn to acting out in the classroom as a way of receiving attention. In these cases, the student may feel that negative attention, in the form of discipline by the teacher, may be better than no attention at all.

Emotional Indicators

Teachers and school staff members should be alert to changes in a student's mood and affect. Some of the emotional indicators that students who experience bullying display include sadness, tearfulness, depression, and anxiety. Through the repeated and demoralizing abuse they face, these students often have very low self-esteem and very low levels of self-worth. Their moods may swing frequently and seemingly unpredictably in line with the frequent and unpredictable amounts of abuse they experience.

Students who are bullied may be afraid to go to school because they fear a recurrence of abuse. As we learned in chapter 1, one of the key components of bullying behavior is that it is repeated. If the abuse is occurring on the school bus, students may be fearful of riding the bus. If the abuse is happening during their walk to school, they may become afraid of the walk or take an unusual route to school to avoid abusive peers. Many times, this alternate path to school is much longer than their normal, direct route to school.

Students who feel they have no other option for ending the violence against them may talk about running away. In addition, they may threaten violence toward themselves or toward others. Thoughts of

F.A.Q.

Teachers often wonder, "Isn't it normal for some students to be left out of activities? Is that really bullying?" Social isolation and exclusion can have devastating effects on students, including affecting their ability to learn. It is very important to encourage students to be inclusive when engaging in social activities. While students will certainly develop friendship groups and hang out with regular groups of people, students who are consistently being excluded from their peer groups should be supported. Teachers can hold classroom discussions about exclusion and encourage students to problem-solve ways to include everyone in activities, which will have a positive impact on students' learning.

suicide and homicide are common among people who feel utterly hopeless and helpless to change their situation.

Behavioral Indicators

Students who are being bullied oftentimes try to avoid the situations in which the abuse occurs. If it is happening at school, students may complain of headaches, stomachaches, and other physical ailments in order to be sent to the nurse's office (and away from the abusive setting). School nurses should be alerted to potential bullying problems if they have students who have frequent somatic complaints without other symptoms of illness. Students who display body language in which they hang their head, hunch their shoulders, and avoid eye contact may also have experienced bullying from their peers. Similarly, students who appear very tired or who cannot seem to stay awake in class may be having difficulty sleeping at night. Changes in eating and sleeping patterns can also be a sign that someone is being bullied.

Academic Indicators

Students who are constantly worried about when and where the next abuse will occur have little energy to concentrate on their academic schoolwork. Students who show little interest in school or schoolwork may be experiencing bullying. Students who are being bullied may begin to receive declining grades, so if a student suddenly begins to do poorly in school when he received good grades in the past, it may be an indicator that something has happened in that student's life. If the abuse is happening in a particular classroom, the student may make attempts to avoid that class. Students who show a loss of interest in extracurricular activities out of the blue may also be experiencing abuse.

INTERVENTION STRATEGIES FOR STUDENTS WHO ARE BEING BULLIED

First of all, if an adult directly witnesses a student being bullied, he should step in and stop the behavior. Chapter 3, "Students Who Bully: Ways to Change Behavior," outlines various on-the-spot intervention strategies that should be used when a staff member witnesses bullying behaviors.

Once the immediate danger of bullying has passed, adults should provide support to students who have been bullied. The U.S. Department of Health and Human Services has a tip sheet called "Providing Support to Children Who Are Bullied: Tips for School Personnel and Other Adults" (stopbullyingnow.hrsa.gov/HHS_PSA/pdfs/SBN_Tip_18.pdf). It provides adults with the tools they need to help students who are

Warning Signs Indicating Possible Bullying

Please check each of the following indicators for the student you suspect may be bullied. Students who are displaying these warning signs may be experiencing bullying (although these can be signs of other concerns as well). Students who are experiencing one or more of these signs or symptoms should be referred to an appropriate adult at school (for example, a school counselor, a teacher with whom he/she feels close, or a school nurse) and the concerns should be thoroughly investigated.

Physical Signs

- ☐ Student's clothing is torn, ripped, and/or dirty
- ☐ Student reports damaged, missing, or lost personal belongings (such as books)
- ☐ Student has unexplained cuts, bruises, or scratches on his/her body
- ☐ Student complains of headaches, stomachaches, or other physical ailments
- ☐ Student appears very tired or sleepy at school
- ☐ Changes in student's eating patterns are visible
- ☐ Student is picked on by other students
- ☐ Student is caught bringing protection (such as a weapon) to school
- ☐ Student is observed hanging head, hunching shoulders, or avoiding eye contact

Social Signs

- ☐ Student has few, if any, friends
- ☐ Student withdraws from social activities
- ☐ Student is socially isolated
- ☐ Student has poor social skills
- ☐ Student begins acting out in the classroom

Emotional Signs

- ☐ Student appears sad, tearful, or depressed
- ☐ Student is displaying symptoms of anxiety
- ☐ Student appears to have low self-esteem
- ☐ Student's moods seem to swing
- ☐ Student is afraid to go to school
- ☐ Student is fearful of riding the bus
- ☐ Student is afraid to walk to and from school
- ☐ Student takes an unusual route to school to avoid peers
- ☐ Student is fearful of joining social groups at school
- ☐ Student talks about running away
- ☐ Student threatens violence toward self
- ☐ Student threatens violence toward others

Academic Indicators

- ☐ Student shows little interest in school or schoolwork
- ☐ Student suddenly begins doing poorly in school
- ☐ Student's grades are declining
- ☐ Student avoids certain classes
- ☐ Student has little or no interest in extra-curricular activities that he/she previously enjoyed

This handout may be reproduced for educational, noncommercial uses only (with this copyright line). From *The Right to Be Safe: Putting an End to Bullying Behavior* by Cricket Meehan, Ph.D. Copyright © 2011 Search Institute®, Minneapolis, MN; 877-240-7251 ext. 1; www.search-institute.org. All rights reserved.

being bullied and to create a healthy, safe climate in their classrooms and schools. Some of the strategies they recommend are as follows:

- Once the immediate threat of bullying has passed, offer support in private to the child who has been bullied. Children often worry that they will "lose face" with their friends and peers if adults are observed coming to their rescue in public.

- Talk with the student who is being bullied to learn what is going on. Explain that the information will be confidential and the student will not be identified to the student(s) who is(are) bullying him. Ensure that the student understands that only the facts about the problematic bullying behavior will be discussed with those involved. Ask about the facts (who, what, where, when, and how) regarding the bullying situation, and have the student describe what positive actions he used to try to stop the bullying. Understand that this may be a very difficult topic for the student to talk about.

- Corroborate the student's experiences with other witnesses. These could be friends, peers, and other adults in the building who are familiar with the student and who may have noticed warning signs or witnessed bullying events.

- Make sure that the student who was bullied understands that what happened is not her fault and that you are sorry that she had to experience the abuse.

- Let the student know that he is being brave to share his story and that you are there to support him. Some students may need to vent their feelings about being bullied and others may need assistance in developing social skills that can assist them in being assertive, building their self-esteem, or identifying friends or peers who can give them support.

- Ask the student what she needs to feel safe and follow through on providing that support to the student. Help the student develop an action plan for staying safe. The action plan should explicitly detail what will be done to help keep the student safe from harm, such as having an adult keep a vigilant watch on things, identifying a peer buddy to support the student, and other steps.

- Communicate the details of the action plan to other staff members in the school building. All anti-bullying policies and procedures should be followed. Encourage other staff members to continue to observe the student who has been bullied and note any concerns they may have. Please see chapter 8 for additional information about schoolwide policies and procedures to stop bullying.

- Encourage the student to report any further incidents of bullying. Students may be concerned about retaliation from the student or students abusing them, so it is important to let them know how this will be handled.

- Encourage the student to develop a close network of friends on whom he can rely. Please refer to chapter 4 for specific information about strategies that bystanders or friends of the student who is being bullied can use to keep their friend safe.

- Involve the student's parent(s)/guardian(s) and offer them concrete ways that they can be supportive to their child. Chapter 7 offers additional suggestions for partnering with parents/guardians to stop bullying.

- If needed, make the appropriate referrals to ensure that the student who has been bullied receives the support that she needs. Experiencing bullying can create psychological, physical, and academic problems for students who are bullied. Please see the "Mental Health and Support Services Referrals" section of this chapter for additional information.

- Most important, follow up with the student who has been bullied to make sure that he knows you are offering your support in the long term. Check in with the student on a regular basis to find out how things are going. If needed, intervene to end any new bullying situations.

CASE EXAMPLES

In chapter 1, we were introduced to Jenny, Ethan, and Ben: three students who were bullied by their peers. In this section, we will revisit each of their stories and highlight concrete, tangible steps that their teachers and other adults in their school buildings could have taken to support them and stop their abuse. Please refer to chapter 1 for their entire case stories.

Jenny's Story

As you may remember, Jenny was a popular student on the cheerleading squad whose friends turned against her when she distanced herself from them after they began making mean and disparaging comments to other students. The more Jenny distanced herself from their bullying behaviors, the more her three friends turned to her as a target of their abuse. Jenny began to fear that her former friends might harm her and she displayed some of the warning signs of being bullied, such as:

- *Change in friendships:* Jenny stopped hanging out with her friends and began associating with other classmates. She avoided her former friends outside of class and at cheerleading events.

- *Change in eating patterns:* Jenny stopped eating lunch with her former friends and began eating lunch with members of the school orchestra instead.

- *Physical signs* from the attack: Jenny exhibited bruises, wet hair, and wet clothing.

- Following the attack, Jenny *skipped classes* for the rest of the day and went home.

- *Change in extracurricular activities:* Jenny skipped cheerleading practices.

Jenny's teachers and other adults in the school building likely noticed some, if not all, of the warning signs listed above. Unfortunately, they did not take action. Below are some suggestions for tangible, concrete, and helpful steps that these adults could have taken to help support Jenny:

1. Once Jenny skipped classes, her teachers could have asked to talk with her in private. During those conversations, they could have asked her about any reasons she had for skipping her classes and encouraged her to talk about what brought on her change in behavior (that is, changing from regularly attending classes to skipping them). Jenny's teachers could have told her that they were concerned about this unusual behavior and that they wanted to help her.

2. Each of Jenny's teachers could have consulted with one another to see if the same behavior (that is, skipping class) was being observed in her other classes. By identifying a pattern of behavior, they could have provided a united front and demonstrated a shared concern for Jenny's welfare.

3. Anyone who noticed the change in Jenny's friendship behavior could have been alerted to a possible problem. Oftentimes when students are having difficulties with their peers, their friendship circles change. A caring adult could have asked Jenny about this change and offered support.

4. Adults who were present in the lunchroom may have noticed that Jenny stopped eating with her former friends and began eating with another group of students. Again, this change could have alerted adults to a possible problem, and they could have

asked Jenny about this. Similarly, Jenny's new group of friends might have been able to provide some insight into this change.

5. On the day of the attack, anyone who witnessed Jenny's bruises, wet hair, or wet clothing should have been immediately alerted to the problem and taken the appropriate actions. The concerned adult could have offered Jenny support and referred her to the school counselor, a school nurse, or a school administrator if she needed additional assistance.

6. When she began skipping cheerleading practice, Jenny's coach could have called Jenny or her parents to find out why she was not attending practice. It is likely that the coach would have observed changes in Jenny's friendship circle as well, especially since some of the mean behavior was occurring during practice.

7. All the adults in this scenario could have talked with Jenny to find out what was happening, helped her develop an action plan to stop the abuse, and provided support. Each of the adults could have followed up with Jenny to see if the solutions were working or if she needed additional support.

Ethan's Story

Ethan is the student in grade 3 who was diagnosed with Asperger syndrome, ADHD, and possible Tourette syndrome. His peculiar behavior made him a target of teasing from his classmates. Some of the warning signs that Ethan was being bullied included:

- *Being picked on* by other students.

- Having *very few friends* in the classroom.

- *Being socially isolated* from the other students.

- Having *poor social skills*.

- *Acting out* in the classroom setting.

Ethan's teacher was well aware that he was a unique and peculiar child. His differences kept him socially isolated from the other students in the classroom and identified him as a target for potential bullies. Below are some suggestions for tangible, concrete, and helpful steps that Ethan's teacher could have taken to help support him:

1. Ethan's teacher could have held classroom discussions with all the students about various ways that people are different from one another and led a discussion on how we can accept others'

differences while respecting them as unique and individual people. In Ethan's case, his parents and teacher did this and it proved very successful.

2. The teacher could have enforced anti-bullying rules and made sure to identify the types of behavior that are unacceptable. In this case, teasing was the main form of bullying, and the entire class could have had a discussion about why teasing behavior is unacceptable.

3. Social skills training for students who are in need of developing age-appropriate skills can be very helpful. Ethan could have been referred to the school counselor or administrator to find out what options were available in his district for students with social skills needs.

4. Creating opportunities for partnerships and friendships among the students can foster a positive classroom climate. Oftentimes when other students get to know students who are different from them, they realize that they have more in common than they thought. By connecting Ethan with his peers, the likelihood of bullying behavior was greatly reduced.

Ben's Story

Remember Ben? He is the student who had five surgeries on his feet and legs throughout middle school. As a result of his medical condition, he became the target of teasing, name-calling, and physical and social bullying at his school. Ben displayed many of the warning signs of being bullied:

- *Being picked on and teased* by his classmates.

- *Being pushed* out of his wheelchair.

- *Physical bullying,* like being slapped.

- *Being socially isolated* by his peers on Xbox.

- Symptoms of *depression.*

- *Mood swings.*

Ben's abuse happened over a period of four years. It is quite likely that his teachers and other adults in the school building noticed some, if not all, of the warning signs listed above, but unfortunately, no one took action. Below are some suggestions for tangible, concrete, and helpful steps that these adults could have taken to help support Ben:

1. Throughout middle school, Ben endured many surgeries and recoveries. His teachers were aware of this and could have identified him as a potential target for abuse. Any adult who witnessed or was aware of the physical bullying and saw him being pushed out of his wheelchair should have intervened immediately to stop the abuse.

2. Teachers could have engaged classes in discussions about people's experiences that make them different (like Ben's medical condition) and about respecting others despite those differences.

3. Anyone who noticed mood changes in Ben (depression or mood swings) could have referred him to the school nurse or counselor or contacted his parents to alert them to this concern.

THE ROLE OF A CARING TEACHER

Positive relationships between students and teachers can have long-term positive effects on students' academic achievement and social and emotional development. Some of the indicators of a positive teacher-student relationship include low levels of conflict, high levels of closeness and support, and low levels of dependency. Students who have positive relationships with their teachers are less likely to avoid school, more self-directed, more cooperative, more engaged in learning, and less lonely, and they like school more and perform better academically. These students have better social skills compared with students who do not have as positive a relationship with their teacher.

According to the American Psychological Association's "Improving Students' Relationships with Teachers to Provide Essential Supports for Learning: Teacher's Module," teachers who have positive relationships with their students do the following:

• Show their pleasure and enjoyment of students.

• Interact in a responsive and respectful manner.

• Offer students help in achieving academic and social objectives (for example, answering questions in a timely manner and offering support that matches the children's needs).

• Help students reflect on their thinking and learning skills.

• Know and demonstrate knowledge about individual students' backgrounds, interests, emotional strengths, and academic levels.

• Seldom show irritability or aggravation toward students.

The APA recommends that teachers develop positive relationships with their students. Make an effort to get to know each student personally, calling her by name and understanding her unique needs to be successful in school. Spend individual time with each student, especially those who are difficult or shy. Provide students with implicit and explicit expectations that you expect them to succeed, making sure your actions and your words reflect those expectations. Encourage your students to have positive relationships—not only with you, but with one another as well. This will help increase the positive climate of your classroom.[1] For more information about teacher-student relationships, please refer to chapter 5. For more information about developing a positive school climate, please refer to chapter 6.

MENTAL HEALTH AND SUPPORT SERVICES REFERRALS

Students who are experiencing emotional distress (related to being bullied or for other reasons) should be referred to their school's mental health specialist/counselor. If there is not a counselor available at the school, the student and his family should be provided with a referral to a mental health specialist in the local community.

The following are two examples of mental health referral forms. The first is from the Arkansas Department of Education's School-Based Mental Health Network. In addition to basic demographic information, it includes all services provided in the last year; the nature and description of the academic, developmental, and/or behavioral problem(s); and the name of the person making the referral. The second form is from the National Assembly on School-Based Health Care's Mental Health Planning and Evaluation Template. It includes the student's name and grade, the name of the person making the referral, the reason for concern, parent/guardian contact information, and a rating of the urgency of the current concern.

Note

1. American Psychological Association (APA) (2010). "Improving students' relationships with teachers to provide essential supports for learning: Teacher's modules." Retrieved September 27, 2010, from apa.org/education/k12/relationships.aspx.

School-Based Mental Health Services Referral Form

Student's Name: _____ DOB: _____ ☐ Male ☐ Female

School: _____ Grade: _____ Teacher: _____

Legal Guardian: _____ Relationship to Student: _____

Street Address: _____ City/State/ZIP: _____

Home Phone: _____ Work Phone: _____

Check all that apply in the last year:

☐ Special Education ☐ Regular Education ☐ 504 ☐ Court Involvement

☐ Outside Agency Involvement ☐ School Counseling ☐ Residential/Hospitalization

☐ Other _____

Nature of Concern:

☐ Behavioral ☐ Academic ☐ Home ☐ Peer ☐ Follow-up ☐ Crisis Intervention

Description of academic, developmental, and/or behavioral performance that prompted the referral

Person Making Referral: _____

Relationship to Student: _____

Date: _____

Sample referral form from the Arkansas Department of Education's School-Based Mental Health Network

This handout may be reproduced for educational, noncommercial uses only (with this copyright line). From *The Right to Be Safe: Putting an End to Bullying Behavior* by Cricket Meehan, Ph.D. Copyright © 2011 Search Institute®, Minneapolis, MN; 877-240-7251 ext. 1; www.search-institute.org. All rights reserved.

Confidential Referral Form

Student's Name: _____

Grade and Homeroom: _____

Referral Source: _____ Date: _____

I would like to refer the above student for evaluation and counseling. I am concerned about the following (please document any specific changes in attitude, appearance, etc.):

Parent/Guardian Name: _____

Phone Number: _____

Please rate the urgency of this request:

Not urgent   Moderately urgent   Very urgent

1   2   3   4   5   6   7   8   9   10

================== (To be completed by clinician) ==================

Date received: _____

Phone call to parent/guardian:

Sample referral form from the National Assembly on School-Based Health Care's
Mental Health Planning and Evaluation Template

This handout may be reproduced for educational, noncommercial uses only (with this copyright line). From *The Right to Be Safe: Putting an End to Bullying Behavior* by Cricket Meehan, Ph.D. Copyright © 2011 Search Institute®, Minneapolis, MN; 877-240-7251 ext. 1; www.search-institute.org. All rights reserved.

CHAPTER 3

Students Who Bully: Ways to Change Behavior

I was a bully because it was the cool thing to do.

—TROY, MIDDLE SCHOOL STUDENT

As we learned in chapter 1, bullying behavior involves an imbalance of power and control. The student who is bullying has distinctly more power than the student being targeted. Power can come in many forms, such as physical strength and prowess, social status and popularity, intellectual level, sports ability, talent, and social skills. Students who bully are able to use their enhanced power in ways to dominate and control their peers. The following table identifies possible ways that controlling behavior is used in each of the above-mentioned power differentials.

For most students who bully, feeling powerful and in control is a very strong reinforcement to continue engaging in that behavior. Some students find enjoyment in bullying others because they like to dominate others in a negative way. They may gain satisfaction from inflicting injury and suffering. They may receive reinforcement for bullying others in the form of prestige, possessions, and/or attention from peers.

WAYS OF CONTROLLING BASED ON FORMS OF POWER

FORMS OF POWER	WAYS OF CONTROLLING
Is physically stronger, has greater physical prowess	Physically intimidating peers, physically assaulting peers
Is more popular, highly regarded socially, known as the cool kid or the funny kid	Spreading rumors that peers will take seriously due to one's social status
Is smarter, has higher intellectual levels	Using wit and intelligence to belittle peers
Is better at playing sports	Physically dominating peers during sports
Has more talent of some kind (musical, speech/drama, dance)	Outshining and belittling peers
Is more skilled socially, has good communication skills, has good relationship skills	Is able to get peers to do things, is adept at manipulating relationships

COMMON MYTHS ABOUT STUDENTS WHO BULLY

Myth: Children who bully are loners.

Children who bully typically have larger groups of friends than other children. Students who bully are quite adept at controlling and manipulating social relationships. Students who bully demonstrate more leadership skills than their peers, but they unfortunately use those leadership skills to engage in abusive behavior. The segment of their friendship group that they control usually supports and encourages the bullying behavior.

Myth: Children who bully have low self-esteem and are insecure.

According to research, students who engage in bullying behavior tend to have average or above-average self-esteem.[1] These are students who are very skilled at controlling and manipulating social relationships and are typically quite secure in their skills.

Myth: Children bully others because they want attention.

Power and control are the two main motivations for students to engage in bullying behavior. Although they may receive attention as a

NOTE Although these common myths have been debunked by research, it is important to note that students who bully are not a heterogeneous group and there are always exceptions. Students who bully may not fit into traditional roles.

by-product, attention in and of itself is not the motivating factor. This is demonstrated by the fact that bullying behavior usually does not stop if adults or other peers ignore it.

Myth: Bullying is just kids being kids. It is a normal part of growing up.

Abusing other people is not a normal part of childhood development and should be taken very seriously. If a child experiences positive reinforcement for abusing other people, the behavior will continue. Many times, children who bully become adults who bully. It is not something that is outgrown. Research has demonstrated that 60 percent of children who bully in school have at least one criminal conviction by the time they are 24 years old.[2]

Myth: Only boys bully.

Girls are just as likely as boys to bully their peers. Both boys and girls can engage in all the different types of bullying, but the percentages of each type may be somewhat different for each group. For example, girls are much more likely to engage in relational bullying while boys are more likely to physically bully other people.

INDICATORS OF BULLYING BEHAVIOR

Physical Indicators

In some cases, bullying is physical in nature. Typically, students who are physically bullying their peers are stronger and/or larger than fellow classmates. An example of this is Trevor, whom we met in chapter 1. Trevor's physical growth spurt occurred sooner than those of his peers, and he used his size and strength to physically torment other students.

Social Indicators

Students who engage in bullying behavior oftentimes have social indicators. They may find enjoyment in controlling others. Sometimes students who bully others are the more popular kids in the class. They may display arrogance and boastfulness and equate "respect" with fear. These students tend to have little empathy or compassion for others. They may be unable or unwilling to see things from another person's perspective. When confronted about their problematic bullying behavior, these students may defend their own actions by insisting it was the other person's fault or simply blame the other person for what happened. They may interpret others' actions as hostile and test authority by pushing the limits. They may be reinforced by others through negative attention. In some cases, they may lack social skills and have difficulty fitting in, although in many cases they have a group of friends they are able to control. These students usually view violence in a positive way.

Emotional Indicators

Some of the emotional indicators that can be a sign that a student is bullying include enjoying feeling more powerful than others; deriving satisfaction from others' discomfort, pain, or fear; displaying little emotion when discussing one's part in the conflict; showing little remorse for negative behaviors; being equally satisfied with negative and positive attention; having a strong self-esteem; being concerned with one's own pleasure and well-being; having poor coping skills; being hotheaded; and getting easily frustrated.

Behavioral Indicators

Some of the behavioral characteristics of students who bully are that they like to dominate and manipulate their peers. They can be impulsive, competitive, poor losers, and attention seekers. Many of these students are good at hiding their negative behaviors so adults will not notice them. Overall, these students enjoy conflicts and refuse to accept personal responsibility for negative behaviors. They will tell lies to avoid consequences for their actions and will attack others before they can be attacked. They have little regard for school and class rules and can be defiant and oppositional toward authority figures. In some cases they may express antisocial traits and aggressive behaviors. Some students who bully tend to get into frequent fights and carry weapons. They may have problems at home. They may use alcohol, tobacco, and other drugs.

Academic Indicators

Students who bully often have problems at school. Because they are very likely to get in trouble at school, they often skip classes. In some cases, these students have very little connection with school and may drop out.

Warning Signs Indicating Possible Bullying Behavior

Please check each of the following indicators for the student who you suspect may be bullying others. Students who are displaying these warning signs may be engaging in bullying behavior (although these can be signs of other concerns as well). Students who are experiencing one or more of these signs or symptoms should be referred to an appropriate adult at school (school counselor, principal, school behavior specialist) to determine if they are bullying and if disciplinary consequences are necessary.

Characteristics

- ☐ Student enjoys feeling more powerful than others
- ☐ Student enjoys controlling others
- ☐ Student is dominating over peers
- ☐ Student manipulates peers
- ☐ Student is popular
- ☐ Student is physically stronger/larger than peers
- ☐ Student is impulsive
- ☐ Student is competitive
- ☐ Student is a poor loser
- ☐ Student is arrogant and/or boastful
- ☐ Student derives satisfaction from others' discomfort, pain, or fear
- ☐ Student equates "respect" with fear
- ☐ Student has little empathy for others
- ☐ Student has little compassion for others
- ☐ Student is unable/unwilling to see things from another person's perspective
- ☐ Student defends own actions by insisting it was the other person's fault
- ☐ Student is good at hiding negative behaviors so adults will not notice them

- ☐ Student enjoys conflicts
- ☐ Student displays little emotion when discussing own part in conflict
- ☐ Student blames others for problems
- ☐ Student refuses to accept personal responsibility for negative behaviors
- ☐ Student shows little remorse for negative behaviors
- ☐ Student lies to avoid consequences for actions
- ☐ Student attacks others before they can attack him/her
- ☐ Student interprets others' actions as hostile
- ☐ Student tests authority by pushing the limits
- ☐ Student disregards school rules and class rules
- ☐ Student is defiant and oppositional toward authority figures
- ☐ Student seeks out attention
- ☐ Student enjoys negative attention just as much as positive attention
- ☐ Student attracts negative attention from others
- ☐ Student is street smart; has strong self-esteem

- ☐ Student is mainly concerned with own pleasure and well-being
- ☐ Student has antisocial traits
- ☐ Student lacks social skills
- ☐ Student has difficulty fitting into groups
- ☐ Student has group of friends that he/she is able to control
- ☐ Student has group of friends that he/she is able to get them to do what he/she desires
- ☐ Student has problems at school
- ☐ Student has problems at home
- ☐ Student has poor coping skills
- ☐ Student is hot-headed
- ☐ Student is easily frustrated
- ☐ Student's view of violence is positive
- ☐ Student gets into frequent fights
- ☐ Student is sometimes injured in fights
- ☐ Student vandalizes property
- ☐ Student uses alcohol, tobacco, or other drugs
- ☐ Student is truant from school
- ☐ Student carries a weapon
- ☐ Student drops out of school

This handout may be reproduced for educational, noncommercial uses only (with this copyright line). From *The Right to Be Safe: Putting an End to Bullying Behavior* by Cricket Meehan, Ph.D. Copyright © 2011 Search Institute®, Minneapolis, MN; 877-240-7251 ext. 1; www.search-institute.org. Adapted from *The Bully Free Classroom* by Allan L. Beane, Ph.D. © 1999. Used with permission of Free Spirit Publishing Inc., Minneapolis, MN; 800-735-7323; www.freespirit.com. All rights reserved.

PREVENTION AND INTERVENTION STRATEGIES: WHAT DOESN'T WORK

Four commonly used strategies to reduce and/or prevent bullying have been proved to be ineffective against bullying behavior. Those four ineffective strategies are (1) zero tolerance policies, (2) conflict resolution and peer mediation, (3) group treatment for children who bully, and (4) simple, short-term solutions.

Zero tolerance policies do not work because it does not benefit anyone to suspend or expel nearly 20 percent of the student body from school. Remember, nearly 20 percent of students are involved in bullying other students. Zero tolerance policies are ineffective because the threat of severe punishment, such as suspension or expulsion, may actually discourage children and adults from reporting bullying that they observe because they feel the punishment is too severe for the incident that they witnessed. Rather than removing students who bully from a structured school setting (which is what zero tolerance policies do), these students should be allowed to benefit from exposure to positive, prosocial role models, such as adults and other students in their school.[3]

Conflict resolution and peer mediation strategies do not work because bullying is a form of peer abuse and not a conflict between peers of equal power and control. Attempting to bring the two involved parties together in the same room and mediate what happened during the bullying incident may further victimize the student who has been bullied. We know that bullying is never the fault of the person being abused, and we should not expect an abused child to be able to solve his own abuse. For a child who has been bullied, facing the student who has abused him can be very upsetting. Teachers and school staff members who have tried this technique have noted that the student who has bullied often repeats the bullying behavior in the conflict resolution or peer mediation session. The student who has been bullied often feels beaten up and victimized again.[4]

Group treatment for children who bully—such as anger management, skill building, empathy building, and self-esteem groups—does not work because these groups provide students with an audience to which they can brag about their exploits. The other group members, students who may also engage in bullying behavior, will likely serve as role models for one another's antisocial and bullying behavior. Another danger is that this group of students can share lists of students who are easily targeted and abused, putting the students who are being bullied at increased risk of abuse from other peers.

Simple, short-term solutions do not work because bullying is a long-term, often repeated problem. As such, it usually takes a repeated, long-term solution to fully address the dynamics involved in a bullying

F.A.Q.

"Shouldn't I bring the students involved in bullying together and have them work things out?" Bullying has quite a bit in common with domestic violence and spousal/partner abuse. As such, attempting to bring the two involved parties together in the same room and mediate what happened during the bullying incident may further victimize the student who has been bullied. Think about domestic violence for a moment: Would you ever ask a battered and beaten wife to sit down in a room with her abusive husband so they can talk and attempt to work things out? No. We know that abuse is never the fault of the person being abused, and we should not expect an abused child to be able to solve her own abuse. A student who has been bullied can have similar physical, emotional, and psychological wounds as a result of her abuse, which has likely been repeated over a period of time.

culture at a school. One-time school assemblies for students or professional development training for teachers do not adequately teach students and staff how to identify bullying or how to step in and stop it from happening. This requires skill building. Just like with learning any skills, sufficient opportunities to practice and master the skill are needed before it becomes a natural part of the culture.[5]

PREVENTION AND INTERVENTION STRATEGIES: WHAT *DOES* WORK

Now that we have addressed what does not work, it is important to identify strategies that are effective in intervening with a student who bullies others.

Intervening on the Spot

On some occasions, adults at school may witness a bullying situation as it is happening. In these cases, it is very important for the adults to intervene and put an immediate stop to the abuse. School staff members have a responsibility to keep the students in their building safe from harm and abuse. Unfortunately, many teachers and school staff members have never received training on the appropriate way to intervene in a bullying situation. The U.S. Department of Health and Human Services' Stop Bullying Now campaign has an informational article entitled "How to Intervene to Stop Bullying: Tips for On-the-Spot Intervention at School" (stopbullyingnow.hrsa.gov/HHS_PSA/pdfs/SBN_Tip_4.pdf) that provides the following strategies:

- When you witness bullying, immediately stop the bullying. If possible, stand between the student who is being bullied and the student who is bullying to block contact between them.

- Enforce the school's rules against bullying. Calmly but firmly explain that the behavior you witnessed is unacceptable and that you will not allow it to happen.

- Do *not* allow the students involved to argue their case about why this situation was or was not bullying or why their behavior was justified. The immediate goal is to stop the problematic behavior, not to gather all the facts related to the situation. That can happen at a later time when someone at the school follows up with the involved students.

- Support the student who was being bullied in a way that allows him to regain self-control, to save face, and to feel supported and safe from retaliation. Tell the student that you will meet with him in private at a later time.

- Remind any of the bystanders who observed the event that they have a responsibility to intervene appropriately the next time they witness bullying. If anyone was observed trying to intervene, praise that person for her efforts. For those who did not act, provide them with possible strategies for the future (for example, "Maybe you weren't sure what to do. Next time, please tell the person to stop or get an adult to help if you feel you can't work together to handle the situation"). Please note that additional suggestions can be found at the Youth Voice Project: youthvoiceproject.com.

- Impose immediate consequences for the student who was bullying. Please refer to chapter 8 for additional information about developing policies and procedures regarding consequences for bullying offenses.

- Do *not* use conflict resolution or mediation strategies. The student who has been bullied may be further traumatized if he is forced to sit in a meeting with the student(s) who abused him.

Setting Consequences for Bullying Behavior

Students who engage in hurtful, aggressive behaviors should receive consequences for their actions. It is important to have school rules and policies against bullying so everyone is on the same page as to what is permissible and what is not. Please refer to chapter 8 for information about developing schoolwide policies and procedures against bullying. Consequences for bullying behavior should be inevitable, consistent, nonhostile, and escalating. Whenever possible, positive reinforcement should also be used to help the student understand the benefits of alternative, prosocial behavior.

Students who bully should be held accountable for their actions. Oftentimes students who bully will try to minimize or excuse their behavior as something that is not very serious. An example would be: "I only called her a name." Sometimes students who bully try to externalize the cause of their behavior or blame the other student. For example, students may say, "I hit him because he kept staring at me" or "If she wasn't so stupid, I wouldn't have talked about her." It is very important that teachers and school staff help the students who are bullying understand that they are fully in control of their actions and that it is their negative, aggressive, hurtful behavior that is the problem. Brainstorm other possible (positive) behaviors that the student could engage in during future situations.

It may be helpful to connect a student who has engaged in bullying behaviors with an adult or peer who can serve as a positive mentor. This person can help the student understand that there are other ways to interact with people rather than abusing them. The positive

Effective Interventions in Bullying Situations

To intervene effectively in bullying situations, follow these steps:

1. Immediately stop the bullying behavior.

2. Enforce the school's rules against bullying.

3. Do not allow those involved in the bullying to argue their case.

4. Support the student who was being bullied.

5. Remind any bystanders of their duty to help others.

6. Impose consequences for any students who were bullying.

7. Do not ask the two parties to sit down and work out the problem together.

This handout may be reproduced for educational, noncommercial uses only (with this copyright line). From *The Right to Be Safe: Putting an End to Bullying Behavior* by Cricket Meehan, Ph.D. Copyright © 2011 Search Institute®, Minneapolis, MN; 877-240-7251 ext. 1; www.search-institute.org. All rights reserved.

role model may also be able to track the student's behavior and intervene, if necessary. The role model can work toward building genuine empathy, helping the student understand and experience the impact of his behavior. Empathy building can help the student build a conscience. The first step in conscience development may involve young people learning that their own actions can cause them to get in trouble. After reaching that realization, they can begin to appreciate the impact of their actions on others.

A tip sheet on this topic can be downloaded at stopbullyingnow .hrsa.gov/adults/tip-sheets/tip-sheet-27.aspx.

Trevor's Story

Trevor, who was larger and more athletic than his peers, was well thought of by the teachers and staff at his middle school. They elected him Best All-Around Boy during his grade 8 year. Unfortunately, Trevor was known among his peers as a bully who would physically assault, pick on, and tease his peers.

Although Trevor was very adept at hiding his assaultive behavior from teachers and other adults at the school, anyone who witnessed his bullying behavior should have immediately put a stop to it. It is more likely, however, that adults would have learned about Trevor's abusive behavior from the other students in his class. If this were the case, Trevor's teacher should have talked to him about his role in bullying other students. By focusing the conversation on his own behavior rather than that of other students, the teacher could help Trevor understand that he is responsible for his own actions.

If it was determined that Trevor had engaged in harmful, aggressive, and abusive behaviors toward his peers, he should be disciplined appropriately. Consequences for bullying behavior should be part of the established anti-bullying policies/procedures at his school. Please refer to chapter 8 for more information about developing and adopting anti-bullying policies and procedures.

To further help Trevor improve his behavior, he could be matched with an adult who would serve as a positive role model for him. This role model could mentor Trevor and provide him with positive reinforcement when he engages in prosocial behavior. The role model could be vigilant to the types of behavior that Trevor engages in and offer support to steer him toward behaviors that are beneficial to him and his peers.

Notes

1. T. Nansel, M. Overpeck, R. Pilla, W. Ruan, B. Simons-Morton, & P. Scheidt (2001), "Bullying behaviors among US youth: Prevalence and association with psychosocial adjustment," *Journal of the American Medical Association, 285,* 2094–2100; D. Olweus (1978), *Aggression in the schools: Bullies and whipping*

boys, Washington, DC: Hemisphere Press (Wiley); D. Olweus (1993), *Bullying at school: What we know and what we can do,* Cambridge, MA: Blackwell Publishers, Inc.; P. T. Slee & K. Rigby (1993), "The relationship of Eysenck's personality factors and self-esteem to bully-victim behaviour in Australian schoolboys," *Personality and Individual Differences, 14,* 371–373.

2. D. Olweus (1993), *Bullying at school: What we know and what we can do,* Cambridge, MA: Blackwell Publishers, Inc.

3. APA Zero Tolerance Task Force (2008), "Are zero tolerance policies effective in the schools? An evidentiary review and recommendations," *American Psychologist, 63,* 852–862; S. P. Limber (2004), "What works—and doesn't work—in bullying prevention and intervention," *Student Assistance Journal, 4,* 16–19.

4. R. Cohen (2002, February), "Stop mediating these conflicts now! The School Mediator: Peer Mediation Insights from the Desk of Richard Cohen," Electronic newsletter, School Mediation Associates, www.schoolmediation.com.

5. U.S. Department of Health and Human Services (2010), "Misdirections in Bullying Prevention and Intervention," Retrieved February 3, 2011 from stopbullyingnow.hrsa.gov/adults/tip-sheets/tip-sheet-05.aspx

CHAPTER 4

The Role of Bystanders: How School and Classroom Climate Can Make a Difference

Empathy is the emotion that alerts a child to another person's plight and stirs his conscience. It is what moves children to be tolerant and compassionate, to understand other people's needs, to care enough to help those who are hurt and troubled.

—BARBARA COLOROSO, AUTHOR OF *THE BULLY, THE BULLIED, AND THE BYSTANDER*

As you will recall from chapter 1, approximately 30 percent of students are directly involved in bullying. It is very likely that the remaining 70 percent of students have some indirect involvement in bullying behaviors at their school.

HOW BYSTANDERS INCREASE BULLYING BEHAVIOR

Among the different roles that bystanders can play, students who **follow**, **actively support**, **passively support**, and **witness in a disengaged manner** all display behaviors that reinforce bullying behavior.

Some of the ways in which students who **follow** can reinforce bullying include actively engaging in bullying behaviors. They send the clear message to everyone else that they believe bullying is okay. Oftentimes students who follow do not start the behaviors, but they jump in once the behaviors have already begun. They do not see anything wrong with harming their peers. In many cases, they may believe that the student being targeted deserves to be bullied. In other cases, students who follow may be coached by students who bully. In this manner, they are told what to do and follow orders. When engaging in bullying behaviors, students who bully and students who follow usually outnumber the students who are targeted. The larger, abusive group of students holds the power, causing other students to be fearful of them. This dynamic reinforces the abusive behavior of these students, prompting them to continue tormenting their peers, which in turn prompts other students to remain fearful of them.

Students who **actively support** bullying are typically not actively engaging in the bullying behavior but are encouraging the students who bully to continue their abuse. For example, these students may laugh at the events they are witnessing or in some way cheer them on. As the numbers in this group rise, more and more students view bullying as normal behavior that is okay to participate in. Some students feel justified in laughing or cheering because they are not directly engaging in the abusive behavior. They do not view their actions as harmful, and they do not understand that they help create a culture in which bullying behaviors are considered acceptable.

Students who **passively support** the bullying behavior may talk with the students who are actively bullying after the event and congratulate them for their abusive behavior. In many cases, these students are fearful of the students who are bullying and do not want to appear supportive of the student being targeted because they think they may be targeted in the future. In many cases, these students do not openly show support for the bullying while it is going on because they do not want to be disciplined by adults at school. Unfortunately, though, they display behaviors that reinforce bullying long after the actual event has passed. They may talk about the bullying with other friends, reinforcing the idea that bullying is something to be celebrated.

Many students who **witness** the bullying behavior may be disengaged, meaning they neither like nor dislike it. They may feel that it is none of their business and therefore choose to play no part in it. Unfortunately, their lack of action leads to the perception that they condone the bullying behavior. In most schools, students who disengage themselves from bullying make up a large part of the student body. The lack of action of so many students can lead to the perception that bullying is not important enough to talk about or address within the school setting. This can lead to a culture and a school climate in which bullying is accepted as a part of life.

There are many reasons why we should try to change student behaviors, as well as the school climate and school culture, when they support bullying behaviors. Researchers have recently discovered that in classrooms where bystanders reinforce bullying behaviors, the students who are being bullied experience more social anxiety and peer rejection.[1] Other researchers have found that students who engaged in bullying in the past were more likely to support and reinforce bullying behaviors among their peers as a bystander.[2] Students who were friends with the student who was bullying were more likely to engage in the behavior also, or to reinforce it. This leads to a perpetual cycle of students abusing other students, which, as we learned in previous chapters, can lead to a variety of problems among the individuals involved and within the school setting.

HOW BYSTANDERS DECREASE BULLYING BEHAVIOR

Students who **defend** or **possibly defend** other students help create a positive school climate and culture, which leads to decreases in bullying. **Defenders** clearly decrease bullying behavior by actively stepping in and demanding that the behavior stop. They send a clear message to their peers that abuse is wrong and it is everyone's responsibility to do something about it. By supporting the student who is being bullied, the students who defend her show her that she is not alone in her struggle. It should be a goal of teachers and school staff to encourage students to defend other students from bullying so the majority of students fall into this defending category. There is something to be said for strength in numbers, and the more students who actively defend other students, the better.

If **possible defenders** had help identifying the skills they possess that can effectively reduce bullying behaviors, they would likely have the confidence to step in to defend students who are being bullied. These students clearly disapprove of bullying, and this sends a message to others that bullying is not okay. Very few people have been explicitly taught how to step in and intervene in an aggressive situation. As a result, not many of us know the right thing to do during these events. The more skills and confidence that students who dislike bullying have, the more successful they are likely to be in getting it to stop. This will increase the number of students who promote a positive school climate and culture, reinforcing prosocial behaviors. For more information about effective strategies that youth have used to combat bullying, visit the Youth Voice Project at youthvoiceproject.com.

Researchers have uncovered several characteristics of students who are defenders or possible defenders.[3] Girls are much more likely to defend a peer against bullying than boys are, and girls tend to use assertive and positive strategies, such as leading the student who is

F.A.Q.

Oftentimes teachers ask, "Why should I be responsible for teaching students social, emotional, and behavioral skills? My job is to teach them the academic content and standards." They argue that teaching these life skills should be the responsibility of parents, guardians, and family members. Unfortunately, many students come from home environments in which these skills are not taught, and this becomes evident in the classroom setting. Classroom behavioral disruptions, students' inability to concentrate on schoolwork, and students' inability to work effectively in peer settings are some of the challenges that teachers face in their classrooms.

The Roles That Bystanders Play

Researchers such as Dr. Olweus have identified different roles that students who witness bullying can play in a bullying situation. These roles include:

Students who follow: those who take an active part in bullying behaviors but are not the ones who initiated the bullying. Students who follow actively imitate the behaviors of students who bully others. In some cases, they carry out orders to harm their peers from the students who bully. When the students who bully are not around, students who follow usually do not engage in bullying behaviors. These students typically only feel confident enough to abuse their peers with the support of the students who bully.

Students who actively support: those who support the bullying but are not actively involved in it. Students who actively support the bullying may cheer or laugh when they witness bullying. Although they do not engage in the behaviors themselves, these students enjoy watching other students being bullied. In some cases, they may fear that if they do not show support, the students who bully will turn on them and bully them too.

Students who passively support: those who like bullying but do not openly show their support. Students who passively support the students who bully are not openly cheering or laughing when they witness bullying. Instead, they may condone or comment on the bullying at a later time. These students talk about bullying events in a positive light with their friends. In some cases, they may congratulate the students who are bullying later that day.

Students who are disengaged witnesses: those who know what is happening but do not like or dislike it. In general, students who disengage themselves from bullying behaviors believe they do not play any role in them and feel that it is none of their business. Unfortunately, these students also believe that it is not their responsibility to try and stop the abuse.

Students who are possible defenders: those who do not like bullying and think that they should help but do not (possibly because they are too scared or because they do not have the proper skills). Students like this are uncomfortable when they witness bullying and believe that it is wrong to abuse someone else. They wish that the bullying behaviors would stop, but they do not know how to make that happen. In many cases, these students are fearful that they will be bullied themselves if they step in and help someone else. Overall, these students do not have the confidence or skills to effectively intervene in bullying situations.

Students who are defenders: those who do not like bullying and actively try to stop it from happening. In some cases, students who defend other students who are being bullied are successful and get the bullying to stop. In other cases, their attempts to stop the bullying are not successful. At the very least, though, they communicate to students who are being bullied that they are not alone and that someone cares enough to stand up for them. The students who defend others are in a unique position and can be very positive peer role models for their fellow classmates.

This handout may be reproduced for educational, noncommercial uses only (with this copyright line). From *The Right to Be Safe: Putting an End to Bullying Behavior* by Cricket Meehan, Ph.D. Copyright © 2011 Search Institute®, Minneapolis, MN; 877-240-7251 ext. 1; www.search-institute.org. All rights reserved.

being bullied away from the situation. Bystanders are more likely to intervene in cases of physical bullying and are less likely to intervene if there are multiple types of bullying going on. Friends of the student being bullied are more likely to intervene to stop their friend's abuse than are students who are not friends. It could be useful to determine what it is about being female, witnessing physical bullying versus other types of bullying, and being a friend of the student who is being bullied that increases one's likelihood of stepping in as a defender.

CLASSROOM STRATEGIES TO CHANGE PROBLEMATIC BEHAVIORS

The following strategies are designed to be implemented in already existing core content curriculum so that there is no need for additional instruction time. The strategies are also designed to help students master the skills that will allow them to be more successful, both academically and in everyday life.

Classroom Anti-Bullying Rules

All teachers understand the importance of classroom rules and expectations for behavior. Many experts recommend enlisting students to help establish classroom rules at the beginning of the school year, then posting them in the classroom, enforcing them with positive and negative consequences, and reviewing them as needed. Typically, these rules include socially appropriate behaviors that are expected in the classroom setting (for example, following directions, raising one's hand and waiting to be called upon to speak, and being respectful).

In much the same way that general rules are needed, classrooms should have explicit anti-bullying rules. Clearly, there should be rules prohibiting bullying behavior and other abusive behavior toward peers. In addition, there should be an expectation that students try to intervene and help if they witness bullying or have a friend who tells them about being bullied. Rules that encourage students to seek out and tell appropriate authority figures (who should listen and take reports seriously) are useful, as are rules that encourage students to act in socially responsible and positive ways toward their peers.

The following four anti-bullying rules are used in the Olweus Bullying Prevention Program:

- We will not bully others.

- We will try to help students who are bullied.

- We will try to include students who are left out.

- If we know that somebody is being bullied, we will tell an adult at school and an adult at home.

 F.A.Q.

During the 2009 International Bullying Prevention Association (IBPA) conference in Pittsburgh, this author had the pleasure of meeting Dr. Olweus during the Olweus Trainers' Day session.

At that session, this author asked Dr. Olweus the following frequently asked question: "What recommendations would you make to teachers who are in schools where schoolwide efforts, like implementing the Olweus Bullying Prevention Program, are not supported (for financial reasons, time constraints, and other reasons) but who want to prevent and reduce bullying in their individual classroom settings?" Dr. Olweus replied that implementing a schoolwide program yields the best results and should be done whenever possible, but if that is not an option, he recommended that teachers focus on three classroom components proved by research to reduce and prevent bullying: (1) developing classroom anti-bullying rules, (2) discussing bullying-related topics during whole-class meetings, and (3) using role-playing scenarios to raise awareness of bullying issues and practice anti-bullying skills.

Four Anti-Bullying Rules from the Olweus Bullying Prevention Program

1. We will not bully others.

2. We will try to help students who are bullied.

3. We will try to include students who are left out.

4. If we know that somebody is being bullied, we will tell an adult at school and an adult at home.

This handout may be reproduced for educational, noncommercial uses only (with this copyright line). From *The Right to Be Safe: Putting an End to Bullying Behavior* by Cricket Meehan, Ph.D. Copyright © 2011 Search Institute®, Minneapolis, MN; 877-240-7251 ext. 1; www.search-institute.org. All rights reserved.

Similar to developing anti-bullying rules, other programs and curricula ask students to take a pledge that they will not engage in bullying behavior. Students acknowledge their intent to follow the pledge by signing their name. The handout on the next page is the Steps to Respect curriculum anti-bullying pledge.

It may be helpful to adapt these rules or the pledge for your classroom setting. Many teachers have added anti-bullying rules to their existing list of classroom rules. Other teachers have developed two separate sets of rules, one general and one anti-bullying, and still other teachers hand out the pledge for students to sign around the same time that the general classroom rules are discussed. There is no right or wrong way to do this. The most important thing is to remember that students should have clear expectations about what behavior is expected of them while they are at school. Whatever way you choose to address bullying behavior with your students, please keep the following key points in mind:

- Be clear about your expectations for students' behavior.

- Explicitly prohibit bullying behaviors and other hurtful acts.

- Explicitly encourage students to be good citizens (and have a discussion with students to define what being a good citizen really means).

- Keep rules simple and understandable.

- Post school rules and policies.

- Discuss school rules and policies with students and their parent(s)/guardian(s).

- Identify negative consequences for students' bullying behaviors.

- Identify positive consequences for students' prosocial behaviors and help students feel proud of their positive actions.

- Consistently, effectively, and fairly enforce school rules.

Whole-Class Discussions about Bullying Topics

One of the ways in which teachers can raise awareness about bullying issues is through whole-class discussions about these issues. Rarely, however, do teachers have time to hold these discussions with students outside of their regular teaching duties. It is possible, however, to talk with students about important issues while still meeting core academic content standards. Weaving social, emotional, and behavioral lessons into core academic content can make learning these life lessons relevant and meaningful to students. The chart on page 55 gives examples of how anti-bullying-related topics can be woven into the academic curriculum to help students understand their role in anti-bullying efforts.

Steps to Respect Anti-Bullying Pledge

We will not accept bullying at our school.

Our goal is to create a safe, caring, respectful school.

We agree that it is everyone's responsibility to stop bullying.

It is up to each of us to make sure that bullying does not happen.

We will:

- Treat others with fairness and respect.
- Find ways to help others join games and other activities.
- Speak out against bullying.
- Refuse to let others be bullied.
- Report bullying to an adult.
- Refuse to bully others.
- Be responsible bystanders who are part of the solution.
- Help others feel safe and comfortable at our school.

Signed: _____

Date: _____

From the Steps to Respect® curriculum (Lesson 10, Part 2, Transparency 1) © 2001, 2005 Committee for Children.

This handout may be reproduced for educational, noncommercial uses only (with this copyright line). From *The Right to Be Safe: Putting an End to Bullying Behavior* by Cricket Meehan, Ph.D. Copyright © 2011 Search Institute®, Minneapolis, MN; 877-240-7251 ext. 1; www.search-institute.org. All rights reserved.

IDEAS FOR ANTI-BULLYING LESSONS

Discussion Topic	ELEMENTARY SCHOOL	MIDDLE/JUNIOR HIGH SCHOOL	HIGH SCHOOL
Respect	**Language arts:** Develop a list of synonyms for the word *respect* and discuss. **Writing:** Have students write a short story about how they would like others to treat them. Discuss the components of respect. **Social studies:** Present students with behavior words and ask them to organize them into *respectful* and *not respectful* categories.	**Character education:** Identify the key components of respect. **Arithmetic/math:** Conduct a survey using questions about respect and compile the results into a graphic report.	**Music:** Develop respect rules for each of the letters in Aretha Franklin's song "Respect" (R=, E=, S=, P=, E=, C=, T=). **Language arts:** Have students read a short biography of someone they admire. Identify the characteristics they respect about that person.
Telling vs. Tattling/Snitching	**Social studies:** Define *telling* (done to keep someone safe) and *tattling/ snitching* (done to get someone in trouble). Ask students to think through the consequences of each action and develop a list for each type of behavior. **History:** Identify famous historical figures who fit in each category. Discuss their actions.	**Writing:** Have students write a short story about two students, one who told an adult about bullying to keep a friend safe and one who told an adult about bullying to get another student in trouble.	**Language arts:** Have students develop a list of synonyms for telling (with the intent to keep someone safe) and snitching (with the intent to get someone in trouble). **Writing:** Using the lists of synonyms developed above, have students write a story using each of the lists. Discuss the differences in each type of story.
Positive Peer Relationships	**Writing:** Provide students with a fill-in-the-blank story about positive peer relationships using vocabulary words.	**Reading comprehension:** Provide students with a reading assignment about relationships. Ask them to identify all the positive and negative characteristics that are included in the story. Discuss.	**Social studies:** Provide students with some case stories from history. Discuss how each person related to his family, friends, and community. Identify positive relationship characteristics and discuss their importance.
Good Citizenship	**Reading comprehension:** Discuss qualities of a good citizen (such as trust, respect, honesty, responsibility, fairness, compassion, self-control), then read a story and have students identify good citizen traits among the characters.	**Government/civics:** Provide the students with a copy of the Declaration of Independence. Have them identify the reasons that the United States declared its independence from Britain. Discuss how Britain's actions were harmful to the United States and how the United States developed ideas for being a good citizen.	**Character education:** Identify positive citizenship characteristics, such as listening, empathy for others, appropriate body language, and respect. Ask each student to identify how she displays each of those characteristics. Ask each student to identify how she could improve each of those characteristics in herself.
Accepting Others Despite Differences	**Character education:** Identify the behaviors that someone would engage in if he accepted others despite being different from them.	**Music:** Have students write a song about accepting people who are different from them, then have them perform it.	**Arithmetic/math:** Create an anonymous survey questionnaire that asks about experiences (for example, how many students have a family member with cancer? How many students come from divorced families?). Have the class chart the percentages, then discuss the results.

An added benefit of broaching these topics with students is an increase in positive teacher-student relationships. Students will likely feel that their teacher cares for them and may be more willing to discuss with them relevant, important, and meaningful topics that affect their daily lives. Please refer to chapter 5 for more information about developing positive teacher-student relationships.

Role Playing for Skill Development and Mastery

When presented with a bullying scenario, students are often very good at identifying possible solutions or solutions that have worked for them in the past. One way teachers can assist students in developing and mastering skills is to allow students to work through these solutions in a role-play setting. After students identify new skills or strategies that they can use or have used to reduce or prevent bullying, they need time and space to practice those skills so they can master them. Role playing offers a great opportunity for students to learn in a holistic manner. The following five steps will help you use role playing effectively in your classroom setting.

Step One: Identify a bullying scenario. This can be done in multiple ways. For instance, students could identify an actual event that has happened at school. This can be a very powerful way of making sure the situation is relevant and meaningful to the students, but you should be very careful to avoid using names and other identifying information. This is not a place to single out specific students as engaging in bullying behavior or as being bullied. If you are uncomfortable with this approach, stories or videos in which a bullying situation occurs can be used instead.

Step Two: Present the bullying scenario to the class and ask the class for possible solutions to the problem based on their experiences. Identify as many different solutions as possible and have the class vote on their top two or three choices. Teachers may need to redirect students to prosocial solutions if they identify solutions that are forms of aggressive, hurtful behavior.

Step Three: Identify students who will describe a brief version of the bullying scenario and then act out one of the voted-on solutions. Make sure the students understand the rules of role playing: (1) role playing is acting, not real life; (2) role playing should focus on clear and understandable objectives; (3) instructions should be clear and understandable; (4) feedback should be positive, specific, helpful, and given immediately following the role play; and (5) role playing can be stopped and started to allow for suggestions.

Step Four: Have identified students act out the objectives of the role play. Typically, the role play should begin at the point immediately following the identified bullying events, with an acting-out of the identified solutions.

Step Five: Allow the class ample time to provide feedback and to discuss what went well and what could be improved upon during the role play. Focus on solutions to the bullying rather than the acting skills of the students. If needed, allow students to incorporate the suggestions into a second take.

By allowing students to be the leaders in identifying harmful bullying situations that they or their classmates have experienced, in developing the solutions to the problem, and in acting out those solutions, you are allowing them to take ownership of the process and making the exercise real for them. The old adage "practice makes perfect" is certainly applicable here. Role playing creates a safe environment in which students can practice—and perfect—anti-bullying skills.

RAISING AWARENESS OF BYSTANDERS' ROLE IN BULLYING

Classroom Discussions

Classroom discussions in which the entire class spends time talking about anti-bullying topics provide an opportunity for raising awareness and skills development. When students who feel uncomfortable witnessing bullying are given the opportunity to voice their discomfort in the safety of a classroom discussion, other students soon begin to realize that they are not alone in their wish for bullying behaviors to stop. Classroom discussions are a great opportunity for students to brainstorm possible solutions to common bullying situations. Since these ideas come from the students, they are typically relevant and meaningful to them.

The topics listed below are suggestions for possible class discussion. The students in your classroom will be able to identify the concepts that they feel are the most pertinent. Teachers can start a classroom discussion by asking the class to vote on the topic that they would like to discuss that day. The ground rules for the meeting should include: (1) not using specific individuals' names but talking about general issues, (2) keeping the meetings focused on solutions, and (3) ensuring that everyone has a chance to participate.

Bystander Behavior

Classes can discuss each of the six different roles that bystanders can take during a whole-class meeting. Students can identify the possible reasons why a student might choose to behave in a certain bystander role. In addition, students can talk about how bystanders who support bullying can change their behaviors and what they would need to support them in that change. The effective strategies used by bystanders who are defenders can be shared with the entire class so everyone can learn about those strategies and techniques.

Telling versus Tattling/Snitching

Most anti-bullying experts agree that it is important for students who witness bullying or who have a friend disclose being bullied to them to report the bullying to adults who can help. One of the biggest reasons that children say they do not report bullying to an adult is that they do not want to be considered a tattletale or a snitch. In some cases, they do not want to get other students in trouble—perhaps because they fear retaliation if the student exhibiting bullying behavior finds out they told. In other cases, students do not tell because they do not believe that adults will take their concerns seriously or do anything about the bullying.

It can be very important to spend time during class discussing the difference between telling someone that bullying is happening and tattling/snitching on someone. Students should be encouraged to tell an adult when they know that bullying is taking place. The goal of telling an adult is to have the adult step in and intervene to keep the student who is being bullied safe. Telling is all about helping the student who is being targeted and informing people about the problem so they can help.

People who tattle and snitch, on the other hand, have very different goals. In the case of tattling and snitching, the goal is to get a person engaging in certain behaviors in trouble. The focus of tattling and snitching is not on the student who is being bullied but rather on the students who are doing the bullying. Students should not be encouraged to try to get peers they dislike in trouble. Rather, the school culture and classroom climate should encourage students to help out peers who are being targeted to ensure that they remain safe. Asking for help or expressing concern for someone's safety should always be viewed as the right thing to do.

Positive, Healthy Relationships

Classroom discussions about positive and healthy peer relationships can be very helpful in diminishing a bullying climate. Students should be encouraged to identify the relationship characteristics that they value in others. In addition, they should identify how they would like others to treat them. By having explicit conversations with students about treating one another with respect, dignity, and compassion, the classroom climate will improve. Other key concepts to discuss include trust, support, honesty, and fairness.

Brainstorming Solutions to Bullying

When students identify a specific bullying situation that they would like to discuss, classroom meetings can be used to brainstorm solutions that have worked. Students are most likely to identify solutions that they have actually implemented. By working together, the students can work through all the potential barriers to suggested solutions within the safety of the classroom. The solutions that are ultimately developed based on everyone's feedback will likely be ones that nearly everyone can agree are valuable.

SKILL BUILDING TO STOP BULLYING BEHAVIOR

One of the most commonly identified barriers to defending abused peers that students who are possible defenders or disengaged witnesses identify is that they lack two things: (1) the confidence that they will not be targeted in the future by the students who are bullying; and (2) concrete, tangible skills to intervene in a variety of bullying scenarios.

Building Confidence among Bystanders

An important way to build confidence in students is to help them identify what they have done in the past that has helped reduce bullying behaviors and how they have been helped by the actions of others. This type of exploration will reinforce positive, prosocial behaviors among students and help identify effective (real-world) solutions for other students who may not have tried those solutions in the past.

In addition to talking with the entire class about the differences between telling and tattling/snitching, it is important to address the very real concern that students who witness bullying have about retaliation if they tell an adult what they witnessed. Many students are fearful that they will become the next target of students who bully if people find out that they told an adult. This is a legitimate concern, and adults at school need to take it very seriously.

In order to instill confidence in students to report bullying, there must be very clear and enforceable consequences for students who are identified as bullying or otherwise harming others. Adults must take reports of bullying very seriously. If adults ignore or downplay reports of bullying, students will lose confidence in adults' abilities to keep them and their peers safe from abuse. Teachers and other school staff need to identify the policies and procedures that will be followed when reports of bullying are received. Chapter 8 provides detailed information about setting up schoolwide policies and procedures against bullying. Everyone (staff, students, and parents) needs to be made aware of what these procedures are so there are no surprises when bullying is reported.

After a report has been made and the appropriate procedures have been followed to substantiate the accusation of abuse, consequences

F.A.Q.

Many teachers often ask, "What should I do if I don't have the ability to carve out time from my day to hold a classroom meeting about bullying?" Anti-bullying topics and positive peer relationship conversations can occur during regularly scheduled academic time. These topics can be woven into academic core content.

should follow. If the student accused of bullying is found to be responsible, disciplinary procedures should be taken. Chapter 6 provides examples of disciplinary rubrics for bullying infractions. If the investigation of abuse shows that the student who reported it gave an inaccurate account of the events or was perhaps lying, the student should suffer the appropriate consequences. It is very important to make it clear that accurate reports of bullying will be taken seriously but that knowingly false reporting will not be tolerated.

Overall, the most important thing that adults at school can do is to take all reports of bullying seriously and follow school policies and procedures to substantiate the abuse. In cases of substantiated abuse, steps should be taken to protect the students who were bullied and the students who witnessed the bullying. Students who engage in inappropriately aggressive and harmful behavior should be disciplined in a manner that is consistent and fair.

Students' confidence levels will increase not only when adults in the school building take bullying seriously and discipline the behavior effectively but also when they have the skills needed to intervene when they witness bullying. Below are some concrete, tangible skills that bystanders can use to intervene in bullying.

Concrete, Tangible Intervention Skills

Refuse to participate in the bullying behaviors: Students who witness bullying can help by not supporting the abusive behavior in any way. This means not spreading rumors that they hear about other students, not excluding students from activities, not joining in during the abuse, not laughing at other students being hurt, and not cheering on the student who is bullying. In general, students who are defenders or possible defenders are already refusing to participate in bullying. It is important to encourage the rest of the bystanders to do the same.

Similarly, it is important for bystanders to avoid fighting back against someone or confronting someone who is bullying. It is never okay to resort to bullying behavior, even if the other person has already been abusive to someone else. In many cases, this approach will only make matters worse. It is not safe to engage in bullying behaviors.

Tell the person who is bullying to stop: Sometimes, for the bullying to stop, it takes someone standing up and saying that he does not approve of the bullying behavior that he is witnessing. Students who feel safe telling the student who is bullying to stop can say that they do not like bullying and do not think it is funny or cool. When other students see a peer standing up for what is right, it can empower them to do the same thing. As more students are willing to intervene, the anti-bullying climate at the school will become more positive. It should be noted, however, that this intervention can be unsafe if the students who are bullying retaliate against the student who stood up to them or the original student being targeted. For that reason, students should be provided with many alternative supportive behaviors that they can engage in to stop bullying.

Tell a trusted adult what is happening: Ensure that all students understand their responsibility to protect others from harm. Help the students identify adults in the building who can be trusted and who know how to help. Ideally, all adults should be trained in how to intervene in bullying situations, and all adults should know what the school policies and procedures are regarding bullying. Oftentimes, students are afraid to tell an adult because they are not sure that the adult will protect them from retaliation. It is important for teachers and school staff to be willing and able to support students who do the right thing and tell them about bullying.

If no one is available at school, students should find an adult at home or in their community whom they trust and tell that person what they have witnessed so they have someone to support their efforts to stop the bullying. When parents and family members approach the school with concerns about bullying situations, their concerns should be taken seriously. Teachers and parents/guardians can be partners in the antibullying efforts. Please refer to chapter 7 for more information about how to effectively partner with parents/guardians to stop bullying.

Be a supportive friend or ally to the student who is being bullied: During the event, bystanders can be supportive by removing the student who is being bullied from the abusive situation. After the event, bystanders can be supportive by talking with the student who was bullied about what happened. Offering a supportive listening ear can show the student who was bullied that someone cares about him. Always encourage bystanders to tell the student who was bullied that it was not his fault. Bystanders can offer to go to a trusted adult in the building with the student who was targeted to help him talk about what happened.

A wonderful resource for more research-based, practical approaches to helping bystanders understand their role in bullying prevention is Stan Davis's book *Empowering Bystanders in Bullying Prevention* (Research Press, 2007). Davis provides information about social problem-solving skills, teaching students empathy, limiting the rewards of bullying behavior, and building partnerships between students and staff to reduce bullying at school.

Notes

1. A. Kärnä, M. Voeten, E. Poskiparta, & C. Salmivalli (2010), "Vulnerable children in varying classroom contexts: Bystanders' behaviors moderate the effects of risk factors on victimization," *Merrill-Palmer Quarterly, 56,* 261–282.
2. I. Oh & R. J. Hazler (2009), "Contributions of personal and situational factors to bystanders' reactions to school bullying," *School Psychology International, 30,* 291–310.
3. Ibid.

What Students Can Do about Bullying

DON'T:

- Spread rumors.

- Exclude students from activities.

- Join in.

- Laugh at other students being hurt.

- Cheer on the student who is bullying.

- Bully the student who is bullying.
  It is NEVER okay to use bullying behavior.

DO:

- Tell the person who is bullying to stop.

- Tell a trusted adult what is happening.

- Be a supportive friend to the student
  who is being bullied.

- Tell the student who was bullied that it
  was NOT his or her fault.

This handout may be reproduced for educational, noncommercial uses only (with this copyright line). From *The Right to Be Safe: Putting an End to Bullying Behavior* by Cricket Meehan, Ph.D. Copyright © 2011 Search Institute®, Minneapolis, MN; 877-240-7251 ext. 1; www.search-institute.org. All rights reserved.

CHAPTER 5

The Role of Teachers: The Impact of Positive, Caring Adults

What the teacher is, is more important than what he teaches.
—KARL MENNINGER, COFOUNDER OF THE MENNINGER CLINIC

Search Institute has identified 40 Developmental Assets® that serve as protective factors for students. Research demonstrates that the more assets a student has, the fewer problems she has at school, the less violence she engages in, and the less she uses alcohol and other drugs. Three Developmental Assets relate directly to positive, caring relationships with nonparental adults:

- Other Adult Relationships: Young person receives support from three or more nonparent adults.

- Adult Role Models: Parent(s) and other adults model positive, responsible behavior.

- High Expectations: Both parent(s) and teachers encourage the young person to do well.

Teachers and other adults in the school can serve as positive role models for their students, providing them with support and encouraging them to do well.

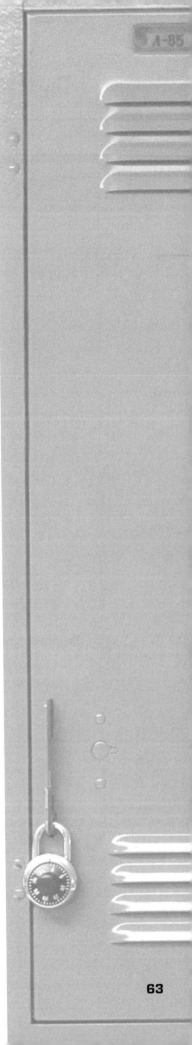

The Framework of 40 Developmental Assets® for Adolescents

Search Institute has identified the following building blocks of healthy development that help young people grow up healthy, caring, and responsible.

EXTERNAL ASSETS

Support

1. *Family Support*—Family life provides high levels of love and support.

2. *Positive Family Communication*—Young person and her or his parent(s) communicate positively, and young person is willing to seek advice and counsel from parent(s).

3. *Other Adult Relationships*—Young person receives support from three or more nonparent adults.

4. *Caring Neighborhood*—Young person experiences caring neighbors.

5. *Caring School Climate*—School provides a caring, encouraging environment.

6. *Parent Involvement in Schooling*—Parent(s) are actively involved in helping young person succeed in school.

Empowerment

7. *Community Values Youth*—Young person perceives that adults in the community value youth.

8. *Youth as Resources*—Young people are given useful roles in the community.

9. *Service to Others*—Young person serves in the community one hour or more per week.

10. *Safety*—Young person feels safe at home, at school, and in the neighborhood.

Boundaries and Expectations

11. *Family Boundaries*—Family has clear rules and consequences and monitors the young person's whereabouts.

12. *School Boundaries*—School provides clear rules and consequences.

13. *Neighborhood Boundaries*—Neighbors take responsibility for monitoring young people's behavior.

14. *Adult Role Models*—Parent(s) and other adults model positive, responsible behavior.

15. *Positive Peer Influence*—Young person's best friends model responsible behavior.

16. *High Expectations*—Both parent(s) and teachers encourage the young person to do well.

Constructive Use of Time

17. *Creative Activities*—Young person spends three or more hours per week in lessons or practice in music, theater, or other arts.

18. *Youth Programs*—Young person spends three or more hours per week in sports, clubs, or organizations at school and/or in the community.

19. *Religious Community*—Young person spends one or more hours per week in activities in a religious institution.

20. *Time at Home*—Young person is out with friends "with nothing special to do" two or fewer nights per week.

INTERNAL ASSETS

Commitment to Learning

21. *Achievement Motivation*—Young person is motivated to do well in school.

22. *School Engagement*—Young person is actively engaged in learning.

23. *Homework*—Young person reports doing at least one hour of homework every school day.

24. *Bonding to School*—Young person cares about her or his school.

25. *Reading for Pleasure*—Young person reads for pleasure three or more hours per week.

Positive Values

26. *Caring*—Young person places high value on helping other people.

27. *Equality and Social Justice*—Young person places high value on promoting equality and reducing hunger and poverty.

28. *Integrity*—Young person acts on convictions and stands up for her or his beliefs.

29. *Honesty*—Young person "tells the truth even when it is not easy."

30. *Responsibility*—Young person accepts and takes personal responsibility.

31. *Restraint*—Young person believes it is important not to be sexually active or to use alcohol or other drugs.

Social Competencies

32. *Planning and Decision Making*—Young person knows how to plan ahead and make choices.

33. *Interpersonal Competence*—Young person has empathy, sensitivity, and friendship skills.

34. *Cultural Competence*—Young person has knowledge of and comfort with people of different cultural/racial/ethnic backgrounds.

35. *Resistance Skills*—Young person can resist negative peer pressure and dangerous situations.

36. *Peaceful Conflict Resolution*—Young person seeks to resolve conflict nonviolently.

Positive Identity

37. *Personal Power*—Young person feels he or she has control over "things that happen to me."

38. *Self-Esteem*—Young person reports having a high self-esteem.

39. *Sense of Purpose*—Young person reports that "my life has a purpose."

40. *Positive View of Personal Future*—Young person is optimistic about her or his personal future.

This handout may be reproduced for educational, noncommercial uses only (with this copyright line). From *The Right to Be Safe: Putting an End to Bullying Behavior* by Cricket Meehan, Ph.D. Copyright © 2011 Search Institute®, Minneapolis, MN; 877-240-7251 ext. 1; www.search-institute.org. All rights reserved.

The Power of Assets

On one level, the 40 Developmental Assets® represent common wisdom about the kinds of positive experiences and characteristics that young people need and deserve. But their value extends further. Surveys of more than 2 million young people in grades 6–12 have shown that assets are powerful influences on adolescent behavior. (The numbers below reflect 2003 data from 148,189 young people in 202 communities.) Regardless of the gender, ethnic heritage, economic situation, or geographic location of the youth surveyed, these assets both promote positive behaviors and attitudes and help protect young people from many different problem behaviors.

0–10 ASSETS	11–20 ASSETS	21–30 ASSETS	31–40 ASSETS

Promoting Positive Behaviors and Attitudes

Search Institute research shows that the more assets students report having, the more likely they are to report the following patterns of thriving behavior:

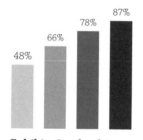

Exhibits Leadership
Has been a leader of an organization or group in the past 12 months.

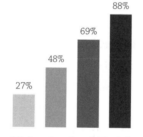

Maintains Good Health
Takes good care of body (such as eating foods that are healthy and exercising regularly).

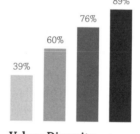

Values Diversity
Thinks it is important to get to know people of other racial/ethnic groups.

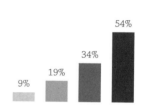

Succeeds in School
Gets mostly As on report card (an admittedly high standard).

Protecting Youth from High-Risk Behaviors

Assets not only promote positive behaviors, they also protect young people. The more assets a young person has, the less likely she is to make harmful or unhealthy choices.

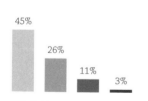

Illicit Drug Use
Used illicit drugs (marijuana, cocaine, LSD, heroin, or amphetamines) three or more times in the past 12 months.

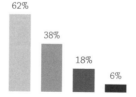

Problem Alcohol Use
Has used alcohol three or more times in the past 30 days or got drunk once or more in the past two weeks.

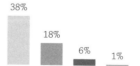

Violence
Has engaged in three or more acts of fighting, hitting, injuring a person, carrying a weapon, or threatening physical harm in the past 12 months.

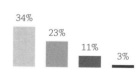

Sexual Activity
Has had sexual intercourse three or more times in her or his lifetime.

This handout may be reproduced for educational, noncommercial uses only (with this copyright line). From *The Right to Be Safe: Putting an End to Bullying Behavior* by Cricket Meehan, Ph.D. Copyright © 2011 Search Institute®, Minneapolis, MN; 877-240-7251 ext. 1; www.search-institute.org. All rights reserved.

THE ROLE OF TEACHERS

Students spend a great deal of time with their teachers, and sometimes their teacher is the most stable nonfamily adult in their lives. Researchers have identified the important role that teachers play in students' lives as "enduring socializing influences."[1] Teachers begin their relationships with students at an early age for the children. This means that teachers have a crucial role to play in students' social development. At the elementary level, students are learning how to navigate relationships with adults, and their teachers are often positive role models and mentors. Teachers demonstrate appropriate adult-child boundaries, respectful relationships, and nurturance and caring for their students. At the middle and high school levels, students are developing into complex social beings, and their teachers can provide them with social support and compassion. Oftentimes middle and high school students struggle with feeling understood by adults, and having a positive relationship with their teachers helps them adjust to these new social relationships.

Teachers spend significant amounts of time with their students. In many cases, a child's teacher may be the only adult, besides the student's parent(s), who sees her on a daily basis. This provides teachers with a unique opportunity to get to know students on a personal level and to have a strong, positive influence on their lives. Teachers are able to notice changes in behaviors, emotions, physical appearance, and/or academic performance. Teachers who have developed positive relationships with their students can support and empathize with them if there are problems they are facing and, in the process, change their lives for the better. In some cases, teachers maintain the relationships for long periods of time spanning several years or more.

First, having a supportive relationship with an adult outside of the immediate family is considered a protective factor that helps young people adapt to adverse circumstances. Children who have positive relationships with teachers have better social adjustment compared to children who do not have supportive relationships with their teachers. This means that these students have someone in whom they can confide about their personal challenges and with whom they are likely receiving well-intentioned advice and opinions. If students face challenges at home, a positive adult outside the home may be the only person in whom they can confide.

Second, positive student-teacher relationships help students develop a strong sense of internal motivation. Having an adult who believes in them, rewards them for taking personal initiative, and celebrates with them as they achieve personal success fosters students' abilities to reach within themselves to try to do their best. This translates to students' willingness to work hard at their academic studies, which leads to higher levels of academic achievement.

 F.A.Q.

Many teachers often wonder, "How does having a positive relationship with my students influence them socially, emotionally, and behaviorally?" These long-term, stable, supportive relationships provide important protective factors to students such as adaptation skills, social skills, internal motivation, personal initiative, active engagement in school, and a sense of belonging.

Third, strong teacher-student relationships are associated with active engagement in school activities. Positive relationships with adults at school foster a strong sense of connectedness with school among students. They help students feel valued and a part of the larger school climate and culture. This sense of belonging and connectedness provides the foundation for meaningful social experiences.

TEACHERS' IMPACT ON STUDENTS' WELL-BEING

Positive teacher-student relationships have a strong impact on children's social, behavioral, and academic adjustment within the context of school settings. Researchers have found that warm, close, and communicative relationships among teachers and students are linked to (1) higher levels of behavioral competence, (2) positive behavioral adjustment, (3) positive school adjustment, (4) positive social adjustment, (5) higher levels of resilience, and (6) better academic achievement among children.[2]

Researchers have identified specific things that teachers can do to promote positive teacher-student relationships, which enhance behavioral, social, and academic adjustment.[3] Specifically, teachers who connect socially to their students and provide them with emotional support help their students thrive. These relationships are typically characterized by warmth, empathy, caring, and compassion for one another. Students who experience such positive adult role models in their lives also experience higher levels of self-esteem and academic achievement, as they have someone in their lives who reinforces their positive traits and characteristics.

Teachers who recognize students' achievements and accomplishments—whether academic, behavioral, or social—protect them against life stress. It is important for teachers to encourage thinking and learning in their students and to let them know that they believe they can learn and succeed. Ensuring that all students feel like they have a chance to participate in classroom activities helps build their confidence and mastery of skills such as critical thinking. When they have high levels of self-esteem, confidence, and mastery of skills, students typically experience more satisfaction with school, are more motivated to do well, have higher levels of math and verbal achievement, are less likely to have behavioral problems, are less likely to drop out of school, and achieve better grades compared to students who do not have close adult relationships at school.

TEACHER-STUDENT RELATIONSHIP-BUILDING TECHNIQUES

In a 2008 study in which he asked students to describe the things teachers do that help them in their lives, Bruce Johnson identified what he described as "the little things" that make the biggest difference in students' lives.[4] These are the social and relationship qualities possessed by teachers who are able to make a meaningful and impactful difference in students' lives.

Being available: Teachers who make themselves available and accessible to students tend to make the most impact on students' lives. In the study, teachers who knew their students very well and showed a sincere interest in their lives were identified by students as positive people. The students felt that their teachers valued them as people and cared not only about how well they did academically but also about all aspects of their lives. A common characteristic of available teachers was that they met with their students regularly to check in and see how they were doing.

Listening: Positive teacher-student relationships were also characterized by teachers who actively listened to their students' concerns and worries and engaged them in a dialogue about what was happening. Students responded the best to open and honest communication with their teachers in which they felt that their teachers really heard and understood them. Students whose teachers listened to them felt that they were being respected.

Teaching the basics: Another thing that students identified as being very important to positive teacher-student relationships was being taught basic academic skills such as reading, writing, and arithmetic. This was especially important for students who had struggled to master these skills in the past. Students who received extra help from their teachers in these areas tended to report positive, healthy relationships with their teachers. By effectively teaching students the core academic skills they need to know, teachers are able to instill confidence and self-esteem in their students.

Being positive: A very important trait for teachers to possess was being able to empathize with their students and understand their life circumstances and to provide them with positive strategies for dealing with adversity. Teachers who encouraged and modeled positive thinking in their students had students with higher levels of engagement and preparedness. In addition, their students developed higher levels of self-esteem and self-confidence as they were able to overcome challenges and barriers through the help and assistance of their supportive teachers.

Intervening: Students found it very important to have teachers who stepped in to help during problematic situations such as bullying, harassment, and social problems at school. Students preferred that teachers actively used their power as adults and professionals to identify concerns and offer solutions. Teachers who acted as caregivers, peacemakers, and effective disciplinarians were highly regarded by students. Students need to feel that their teachers care about them and that they are willing to step in to help them when needed (whether to stop bullying or to support them in something happening in their lives).

Having fun: Students felt more comfortable with teachers who could have fun and tell a good joke while doing the more serious things such as teaching core academic content. Students felt more at ease around teachers who were in control of the classroom but who could keep everyone's motivation levels high by using humor. Humor is a great way to show personal connections with other people, and positive social connections help students feel like they are part of a positive school climate and culture.

Remembering personal events and holidays: Teachers who remembered special events in students' lives, such as birthdays, holidays, and extracurricular activities, were highly regarded by their students. Human beings are social creatures, and acknowledging important events in our lives demonstrates that others see us as important. Sometimes personal events can be a source of sorrow, such as the death of a family member. Teachers who supported students through these difficulties were viewed as caring and special among their students.

Being real: Teachers who were comfortable being themselves around their students promoted prosocial bonding between themselves and their students. This may mean sharing some things that are personal with students, especially if those stories can be used as teachable moments for students. Students sometimes have a difficult time recognizing that their teachers are regular people too. By bringing a bit of yourself into the classroom, you are telling the students that you value them enough to share a part of your life with them. This is very important in fostering positive social relationships. Students need to feel that their relationships with their teachers are reciprocal and not one-sided.

Being respectful: Although they need to remain effective disciplinarians who are in charge of the classroom, teachers should demonstrate as much respect toward their students as they demand from them. Teachers are in a unique position to be positive adult role models in students' lives, and they can show students how to be respectful. Oftentimes if students do not have an adult in their lives who displays respectful behavior, they may struggle to understand exactly what it means to be respectful and why it is important.

The worksheets on pages 72–80 can serve as self-assessment tools to identify the strengths that teachers, as positive adults in their students' lives, possess. After completing the assessments, it may be helpful to identify your strengths as a teacher and to set one or more goals you would like to achieve that could help you improve your ability to connect with your students.

Notes

1. American Psychological Association (APA) (2010), "Improving students' relationships with teachers to provide essential supports for learning: Teacher's modules," retrieved September 27, 2010, from apa.org/education/k12/relationships.aspx.

2. V. Battistich, E. Schaps, & N. Wilson (2004), "Effects of an elementary school intervention on students' 'connectedness' to school and social adjustment during middle school," *Journal of Primary Prevention, 24*(3), 243–262; D. Berry & E. O'Connor (2009), "Behavioral risk, teacher-child relationships, and social skill development across middle childhood: A child-by-environment analysis of change," *Journal of Applied Developmental Psychology, 31*(1), 1-14; S. H. Birch & G. W. Ladd (1997), "The teacher-child relationship and early school adjustment," *Journal of School Psychology, 55*(1), 61–79; B. K. Hamre & R. C. Pianta (2001), "Early teacher-child relationships and the trajectory of children's school outcomes through eighth grade," *Child Development, 72,* 625–638; A. M. Klem & J. P. Connell (2004), "Relationships matter: Linking teacher support to student engagement and achievement," *Journal of School Health, 74*(7), 262–273; C. Murray & M. T. Greenberg (2001), "Relationships with teachers and bonds with school: Social emotional adjustment correlates for children with and without disabilities," *Psychology in the Schools, 38,* 25–41; R. C. Pianta (1994), "Patterns of relationships between children and kindergarten teachers," *Journal of School Psychology, 32,* 15–31; R. C. Pianta, M. S. Steinberg, & K. B. Rollins (1995), "The first two years of school: Teacher-child relationships and deflections in children's classroom adjustment," *Development and Psychopathology, 7,* 295–312.

3. J. Cornelius-White (2007), "Learner-centered teacher-student relationships are effective: A meta-analysis," *Review of Educational Research, 77*(1), 113–143; B. Johnson (2008), "Teacher-student relationships which promote resilience at school: A micro-level analysis of students' views," *British Journal of Guidance & Counselling, 36*(4), 385–398; E. A. Skinner & M. J. Belmont (1993), "Motivation in the classroom: Reciprocal effects of teacher behavior and student engagement across the school year," *Journal of Educational Psychology, 85,* 571–581.

4. B. Johnson, (2008). "Teacher-student relationships which promote resilience at school: A micro-level analysis of students' views," *British Journal of Guidance & Counselling, 36*(4), 385–398.

Availability

*Are you available to your students—not only for their academic needs
but also for their social, emotional, and behavioral needs?*

	YES	SOMETIMES	NO
Do you acknowledge events in students' lives?	☐	☐	☐
Do you ask students how their previous evening was?	☐	☐	☐
Do you ask students what they did over the weekend?	☐	☐	☐
Do you express concern if students have experienced a problem?	☐	☐	☐
Do you ask students how they are feeling?	☐	☐	☐
If students ask for help, do you find time in your day to help?	☐	☐	☐
Are you easily accessible to your students throughout the day?	☐	☐	☐
Do you know each of your students on a personal level?	☐	☐	☐
Do you attend your students' extracurricular activities?	☐	☐	☐
Do you meet individually with your students on a regular basis?	☐	☐	☐
Do you celebrate students' academic achievements?	☐	☐	☐
Do you celebrate students' nonacademic achievements?	☐	☐	☐
When students experience a problem in the classroom, do you offer solutions?	☐	☐	☐

This handout may be reproduced for educational, noncommercial uses only (with this copyright line). From *The Right to Be Safe: Putting an End to Bullying Behavior* by Cricket Meehan, Ph.D. Copyright © 2011 Search Institute®, Minneapolis, MN; 877-240-7251 ext. 1; www.search-institute.org. All rights reserved.

Listening

Are you actively listening to your students' worries and concerns?

	YES	SOMETIMES	NO
Do you allow students to tell you their stories?	☐	☐	☐
Do you let students finish talking before you respond to them?	☐	☐	☐
When talking with students, are you honest with them?	☐	☐	☐
When talking to students, are you open about your feelings?	☐	☐	☐
When talking to students, are you open about your thoughts?	☐	☐	☐
When a student needs to talk, do you find time for him?	☐	☐	☐
Do you make direct eye contact with students while talking?	☐	☐	☐
Do you try to understand what your students are feeling while they are talking to you?	☐	☐	☐
Do you restate what students have said to double-check that you have heard them accurately?	☐	☐	☐
Do you ask students for clarification when you do not understand something that they have said?	☐	☐	☐
Are you aware of your own feelings, thoughts, beliefs, biases, perceptions, and values when talking with students?	☐	☐	☐
Do you summarize what students have told you?	☐	☐	☐
Do you reflect back what you believe the students are feeling and thinking and ask for confirmation?	☐	☐	☐

This handout may be reproduced for educational, noncommercial uses only (with this copyright line). From *The Right to Be Safe: Putting an End to Bullying Behavior* by Cricket Meehan, Ph.D. Copyright © 2011 Search Institute®, Minneapolis, MN; 877-240-7251 ext. 1; www.search-institute.org. All rights reserved.

Teaching the Basics

Are you actively teaching your students basic academic skills such as reading, writing, and arithmetic?

	YES	SOMETIMES	NO
Do you provide extra help for students who are struggling to learn?	☐	☐	☐
Are you providing students with skills to master academic content?	☐	☐	☐
Are you providing regular feedback to students about their progress in their academic studies?	☐	☐	☐
Are you connecting students with academic support services if they are needed?	☐	☐	☐
Are your students confident in their academic abilities?	☐	☐	☐
Do your students believe they can succeed academically?	☐	☐	☐
Do you support peer mentoring in your classroom?	☐	☐	☐
Do you regularly look for sudden changes in students' academic performance and talk with students when they occur?	☐	☐	☐
If students' performance has abruptly changed, do you offer your support and concern to your students?	☐	☐	☐
Do you regularly provide feedback about students' academic performance to their parents and guardians?	☐	☐	☐
Do you often partner with parents and guardians to facilitate homework assignments?	☐	☐	☐
Do you teach academic content using multiple methods?	☐	☐	☐
Do you identify individual strengths among all your students?	☐	☐	☐

This handout may be reproduced for educational, noncommercial uses only (with this copyright line). From *The Right to Be Safe: Putting an End to Bullying Behavior* by Cricket Meehan, Ph.D. Copyright © 2011 Search Institute®, Minneapolis, MN; 877-240-7251 ext. 1; www.search-institute.org. All rights reserved.

Being Positive

Are you being a positive role model for your students?

	YES	SOMETIMES	NO
Do you provide students with positive strategies to overcome difficult situations?	☐	☐	☐
Do you frame situations as opportunities rather than barriers?	☐	☐	☐
Are you engaging with your students?	☐	☐	☐
Do you help your students with preparedness?	☐	☐	☐
Are you able to motivate your students?	☐	☐	☐
Do you model positive thinking with your students?	☐	☐	☐
Do you help students set manageable goals?	☐	☐	☐
Do you promote optimism in your classroom?	☐	☐	☐
Do you appreciate your students' individual differences?	☐	☐	☐
Do you encourage your students to be creative?	☐	☐	☐
Do you encourage your students to use their imaginations?	☐	☐	☐
Are you often smiling in your classroom?	☐	☐	☐
Do you reinforce your students' helpful behavior?	☐	☐	☐

This handout may be reproduced for educational, noncommercial uses only (with this copyright line). From *The Right to Be Safe: Putting an End to Bullying Behavior* by Cricket Meehan, Ph.D. Copyright © 2011 Search Institute®, Minneapolis, MN; 877-240-7251 ext. 1; www.search-institute.org. All rights reserved.

Intervening

Do you help and support students who are experiencing academic or social, emotional, and behavioral problems?

	YES	SOMETIMES	NO
Do you step in if a student is being bullied?	☐	☐	☐
Do you step in if a student is being harassed or intimidated?	☐	☐	☐
When you know about students' social problems, do you try to help?	☐	☐	☐
Do you actively ask students about any concerns that they may be experiencing?	☐	☐	☐
Do you provide students with different solutions for their identified problems?	☐	☐	☐
Are you an effective disciplinarian for your students?	☐	☐	☐
Can you maintain the peace among your students?	☐	☐	☐
Are you aware of the academic supports that are available to your students?	☐	☐	☐
Are you aware of the social supports that are available to your students?	☐	☐	☐
Do you regularly inform your students and their parent(s)/guardian(s) about additional supports that you feel would benefit students?	☐	☐	☐

This handout may be reproduced for educational, noncommercial uses only (with this copyright line). From *The Right to Be Safe: Putting an End to Bullying Behavior* by Cricket Meehan, Ph.D. Copyright © 2011 Search Institute®, Minneapolis, MN; 877-240-7251 ext. 1; www.search-institute.org. All rights reserved.

Having Fun

Do you have fun and enjoy your time in the classroom with your students?

	YES	SOMETIMES	NO
Do you use humor to engage your students?	☐	☐	☐
Do you engage students in fun activities?	☐	☐	☐
Is your classroom a comfortable place to be?	☐	☐	☐
Do students feel at ease in your classroom?	☐	☐	☐
Are you able to maintain control of your classroom?	☐	☐	☐
Do you motivate your students to do well academically?	☐	☐	☐
Do you motivate your students to do well in nonacademic areas of their lives?	☐	☐	☐
Do you feel personally connected to each of your students?	☐	☐	☐
Do your students like to be in your classroom?	☐	☐	☐
Do you enjoy your time in the classroom?	☐	☐	☐

This handout may be reproduced for educational, noncommercial uses only (with this copyright line). From *The Right to Be Safe: Putting an End to Bullying Behavior* by Cricket Meehan, Ph.D. Copyright © 2011 Search Institute®, Minneapolis, MN; 877-240-7251 ext. 1; www.search-institute.org. All rights reserved.

Remembering Personal Events and Holidays

Do you remember and acknowledge personal events that are relevant and meaningful to your students?

	YES	SOMETIMES	NO
Do you celebrate each of your students' birthdays?	☐	☐	☐
Are you aware of special events in your students' lives?	☐	☐	☐
Are you aware of time periods that may be difficult for your students (such as anniversaries of family members' deaths)?	☐	☐	☐
Do you celebrate holidays with your students?	☐	☐	☐
Are you aware of different religious events that each of your students celebrates and honors?	☐	☐	☐
Do you respect students' unique cultural traditions concerning holidays and celebrations?	☐	☐	☐
Are you aware of the various extracurricular activities that your students are involved with?	☐	☐	☐
Do you support your students outside the classroom by attending extracurricular activities or other events they are part of?	☐	☐	☐

This handout may be reproduced for educational, noncommercial uses only (with this copyright line). From *The Right to Be Safe: Putting an End to Bullying Behavior* by Cricket Meehan, Ph.D. Copyright © 2011 Search Institute®, Minneapolis, MN; 877-240-7251 ext. 1; www.search-institute.org. All rights reserved.

Being Real

Do you present the real you to your students?

	YES	SOMETIMES	NO
Are you comfortable being yourself around your students?	☐	☐	☐
Do you share personal stories with your students?	☐	☐	☐
Do you use your own personal stories and examples as teachable moments in your classroom?	☐	☐	☐
Are you honest and open with your students about your thoughts?	☐	☐	☐
Are you honest and open with your students about your feelings?	☐	☐	☐
Are you open and honest with your students about your beliefs and attitudes?	☐	☐	☐
Are you open and honest with your students about your values?	☐	☐	☐
When your students ask you a personal question, do you answer them directly?	☐	☐	☐

This handout may be reproduced for educational, noncommercial uses only (with this copyright line). From *The Right to Be Safe: Putting an End to Bullying Behavior* by Cricket Meehan, Ph.D. Copyright © 2011 Search Institute®, Minneapolis, MN; 877-240-7251 ext. 1; www.search-institute.org. All rights reserved.

Being Respectful

Do you maintain a respectful classroom in which you are respected by your students and respect them in turn?

	YES	SOMETIMES	NO
Do you respect each of your students' uniqueness?	☐	☐	☐
Do you feel respected by each of your students?	☐	☐	☐
Are you a positive role model for your students?	☐	☐	☐
Do you regularly demonstrate respectful behavior toward your students?	☐	☐	☐
Do you discuss respect with your students?	☐	☐	☐
Do you encourage your students to be respectful to one another?	☐	☐	☐

This handout may be reproduced for educational, noncommercial uses only (with this copyright line). From *The Right to Be Safe: Putting an End to Bullying Behavior* by Cricket Meehan, Ph.D. Copyright © 2011 Search Institute®, Minneapolis, MN; 877-240-7251 ext. 1; www.search-institute.org. All rights reserved.

CHAPTER 6

Positive Classroom Culture and Climate

It's basically a fundamental human right for a student to feel safe at school.

—DR. DAN OLWEUS, BULLYING RESEARCHER

Classroom culture refers to the shared ideas, attitudes, beliefs, assumptions, and values that determine expected boundaries and behaviors within the classroom setting. These are things that are deeply ingrained within the classroom and that are often taken for granted. The components that can influence classroom culture are the ways in which the room is arranged and decorated, how teachers and students interact with one another, the common beliefs and values that are communicated and reinforced, and the daily rituals, rules, and procedures of the classroom.

Classroom climate refers to the way that students and teachers feel about their classroom. The components of a positive classroom climate include a welcoming, safe environment that promotes communication, interaction, learning, and a sense of belonging. Research demonstrates that classrooms with appropriate teacher-student ratios and that are orderly, quiet, and well maintained are more conducive to learning than overcrowded, disorderly, noisy, and poorly maintained classrooms.[1] A positive classroom climate can be found in safe, comfortable, and inviting classrooms.

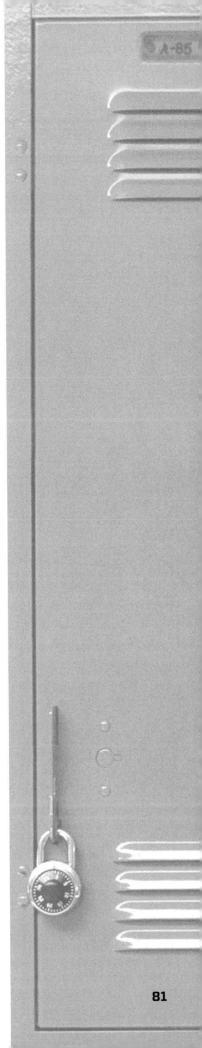

CREATING A POSITIVE CLASSROOM CULTURE

Classrooms that are arranged and decorated to meet the educational and social, emotional, and behavioral needs of students are more likely to have students who achieve academically and socially. Many experts have identified different ways that teachers can arrange students' desks, chairs, and tables in a classroom. The following chart displays four possible seating arrangements: a square, clusters, rows, and a U-shape. These different types of seating arrangements have unique assets and challenges. For example, seating children in several rows facing the teacher's desk at the front of the room provides each student with her own individual space. Students who are seated behind or next to other students, however, have the opportunity to pick on students who are seated directly in front of or to the side of them. This arrangement can also make it difficult for teachers to supervise students who are seated toward the back of the classroom. The chart also discusses potential benefits and drawbacks for each of these seating arrangements.

Classroom decorations can have a significant influence on student behavior. Classrooms that have rules posted in easily visible areas will facilitate students' ability to read and review the classroom rules on a regular basis. The classroom seating arrangement will certainly affect who can and cannot read signage in certain areas of the room. Also, in classrooms with abundant signage, students may be distracted by competing posters and disregard the classroom rules. Additionally, classrooms in which students' accomplishments are prominently displayed promote a higher sense of accomplishment, self-efficacy, and self-esteem among students. Regularly updating students' displayed work will promote students' continued quest for high achievement.

The ways in which teachers and students interact contribute to the classroom culture. Classrooms in which students have an active role in the decision-making process increase students' confidence levels and mastery of critical thinking skills. By allowing students to play a real role in what happens in their classroom, teachers help students take a greater share of the ownership and responsibility for the classroom. This involvement also helps the teachers understand the kinds of things that are relevant and meaningful to their students.

Shared beliefs and values among teachers and students are also very important to the classroom culture. Classrooms in which everyone believes that students can and will be successful are more likely to have students who achieve academically and socially. Effective teachers share a belief that students are able and willing to learn. This attitude helps empower students to strive to be as successful as they can possibly be.

BENEFITS AND DRAWBACKS OF DIFFERENT TYPES OF CLASSROOM SEATING ARRANGEMENTS

Type of Layout	BENEFITS	DRAWBACKS
Square	Students can easily engage in classroom discussions. Everyone is part of a single unit (that is, the square). Students who bully should be placed in a corner of the square as close to the teacher as possible. Students who are being bullied can be placed away from students who have targeted them so they can avoid eye contact and physical contact.	Some students will have difficulty interacting with other students (that is, students who are several desks apart on the same side of the square). If the teacher is not part of the square, he will always have students' backs to him, making it difficult to supervise them.
Clusters	This arrangement encourages small-group work. Students who bully and students who have been bullied can be placed in different clusters where they can avoid eye contact and physical contact. Students who bully should be placed as close to the teacher as possible for increased supervision.	Several members of the small group can gang up on the remaining student. It can be difficult for the teacher to supervise all clusters at the same time.
Rows	In this arrangement, there is less talking, and all students can see the front board in the room. This arrangement works well for lecturing. Students who bully can be strategically placed so that the teacher can easily supervise them.	Students may find it difficult to have meaningful classroom discussions because they cannot face everyone. It can be easy to pick on students in front of or to the side of a student. It can be difficult for the teacher to supervise students in the back of the rows.
U-Shape	U-shaped arrangements foster communication among all students and work well for classrooms of 20 or less. Students who are involved in bullying can be separated to avoid eye contact and physical contact.	Similarly to the square, with a U-shape students will find it difficult to engage students who are seated several desks away from them on the same side.

Daily rituals, rules, and procedures can also support a positive classroom culture. One of the most important things for students is consistency in what is expected of them. Effective teachers consistently behave in ways that students can predict. They reinforce the classroom rules each and every time they are applicable, and they follow the same procedures for all students. This helps students feel a sense of balance and fairness in the classroom setting. It should be noted, however, that positive surprises such as celebrations should not be discarded in order to keep a sense of ritual within the classroom as these celebrations can be very important to teacher-student relationships.

Taken together, all of these components can either support or hinder the classroom culture and learning. It can be difficult to alter some of these things because they may be deeply ingrained and unlikely to be noticed by teachers and students within the classroom. The aforementioned classroom characteristics do, however, warrant an appraisal to determine if any of them may be unknowingly promoting bullying or other harmful behaviors. If so, alterations can be made to begin the process of changing the culture to one that is more prosocial, positive, and caring.

CREATING A POSITIVE CLASSROOM CLIMATE

A positive classroom climate can support communication and interaction among students and teachers. Teachers who are open to students' suggestions and who actively involve students in classroom decision making will communicate to students that everyone is being listened to and respected. In cases of mutual conflict and disagreements, utilizing conflict resolution strategies will help students master those relationship and interpersonal skills. In classrooms with a positive climate, there are higher levels of trust, respect, and caring among everyone in the classroom.

A positive classroom climate creates a sense of community in which everyone in the classroom is valued. Utilizing multimodal teaching methods ensures that students with different learning styles are able to understand the material and thrive in the classroom. Classrooms with a positive climate typically have high expectations for all students.

Researchers have found that a positive classroom climate is correlated with:

• Better academic achievement and higher grades among students.

• Increased engagement and connectedness among students and teachers.

• Higher rates of school attendance among students.

• Higher rates of grade promotion.

- Increased self-image and self-esteem.

- Lower levels of students receiving suspensions.

- Lower levels of depression, anxiety, and loneliness.

- Students who are less likely to drink alcohol, smoke tobacco, or use other drugs.[2]

These positive outcomes foster a shared sense of accomplishment among the members of the class. Overall, students and teachers alike will experience more confidence, pride, self-esteem, and motivation to work harder toward academic and social goals. Unfortunately, though, in classrooms in which the climate is negative, undesirable outcomes may occur.

HOW CLASSROOM CLIMATE AND CULTURE AFFECT BULLYING BEHAVIORS

As we have learned from previous chapters, bullying behavior has three distinct characteristics. It is aggressive and harmful behavior that is done on purpose. It is started by individuals who have more power and control than the individuals who are targeted, and it is usually repeated. We have also learned that everyone plays a role in encouraging or discouraging bullying behaviors, either as someone who is bullying, someone who is being bullied, or someone who is witnessing the bullying.

In a classroom setting, the classroom culture and climate can play a big role in whether or not bullying behavior is reinforced. For example, classrooms that are arranged in a way that allows students to hide their behaviors from their teachers are more likely to encourage problematic behaviors. If students are able to reach out and touch other students or their belongings, this may promote problematic behaviors such as bullying. If students are able to whisper to one another without the teacher being aware, it is more likely that rumors and gossip will be spread in the classroom.

What are considered normal interactions among teachers and students in a classroom can also have an effect on bullying or other aggressive behaviors. In many cases, teachers may not have the skills to intervene in bullying or may not feel confident that they know the right thing to do in cases of bullying or aggressive behavior. As a result, some teachers may resort to ignoring the behaviors in the hope that they will go away on their own. Unfortunately, we know that bullying is a form of peer abuse that is typically reinforced by the silence of those who are present. Simply ignoring the behavior will not keep the student who is targeted safe and will lead to the belief among the students that their teachers condone bullying behaviors. Stated differently, students will recognize that their teachers are not going to discipline them for bullying behaviors, which can lead to additional bullying behaviors in the future.

In all classrooms, there are often unspoken and unexamined common beliefs and values that are communicated to the group. In classrooms in which teachers believe that bullying is just kids being kids, the students will see that bullying does not warrant intervention and discipline from adults at school and that it is therefore okay. Other teachers may value students who stand up for themselves, which may promote the belief among students that they are responsible for taking care of themselves (even in abusive situations such as bullying). Unfortunately, this attitude can be very dangerous for students as they may receive further harm from the students who are abusing them. Remember that the student who is bullying has more power and control than the student who is being bullied.

All classrooms have daily rituals, rules, and procedures that are well understood by students and teachers alike. By maintaining these patterns, everyone in the class knows what to expect throughout the day. This can facilitate a learning environment by providing a predictable series of events throughout the day, but it can also lead to problems. For example, students who are abusing other students will likely have identified those times when they can hide their abusive behaviors from adults or will have more supportive bystanders around who will encourage and celebrate their behavior.

With regard to classroom climate, classrooms that are unwelcoming, unsafe, and do not promote communication, interaction, learning, or a sense of belonging are much more likely to have higher rates of bullying behaviors among the students. Safety and feeling welcome are perceptions and can differ among students and teachers, even in the same classroom. It is important to ensure that everyone feels welcome and safe in the classroom environment. Individuals who do not feel that they can communicate or interact with their teachers are unlikely to let adults at school know if they are experiencing a problem with another student or group of students. It is very important for students to feel as though they belong, and students who do not feel like they belong in the classroom are more likely to be targeted by their peers. As we have learned previously, students who are bullied are often targeted because others choose to exclude or harm those who are different in some way from their peers. In many cases, these students have few, if any, friends, which can lead to a sense of isolation.

Classrooms that are typically disorderly and are not well maintained tend to be more chaotic than orderly, quiet, well-maintained classrooms. Also, if there is a high student-to-teacher ratio, it will be increasingly difficult for the teacher to maintain control of the classroom and keep an active eye on all the students. Students who engage in abusive behaviors toward their peers will capitalize on those opportunities in a chaotic and uncontrolled classroom to further abuse others. This type of classroom environment provides the perfect opportunity for unhelpful reinforcement (for example, bystanders who laugh and cheer or bystanders who join in the behavior) compared to well-controlled classrooms.

CLASSROOM MANAGEMENT

One of the most powerful tools that a teacher can use to deter bullying behaviors is the use of effective classroom management techniques. The following section describes effective and easy-to-use classroom management techniques to reduce bullying at school.

Fostering a Positive Classroom Climate and Culture

Search Institute's 40 Developmental Assets include seven assets that can have a direct impact on classroom climate and culture:

- Asset #3: Other (nonparent) adult relationships

- Asset #5: A caring school climate

- Asset #7: A community that values youth

- Asset #8: A community that sees youth as resources

- Asset #10: A safe environment

- Asset #12: School boundaries

- Asset #16: High expectations

The first asset listed above, having **positive and caring relationships with other adults** who are not the child's parents, was discussed in chapter 5. As you may recall, students who have caring, positive relationships with teachers have better social adjustment, better behavioral adjustment, better school adjustment, higher levels of internal motivation, more resilience, active engagement at school, and better academic achievement. For more information about positive relationship-building techniques that can foster caring teacher-student relationships, please refer to chapter 5. These positive relationships are associated with a more positive classroom culture and climate.

The other six assets can be described as follows. **A caring school climate** is one in which positive character traits such as respect, honesty, determination, and hard work are encouraged. In addition to encouraging positive character traits, a caring school climate is one in which positive interpersonal traits are valued. These traits include helping behaviors, altruism, teamwork, and good citizenship.

Communities that value youth and see them as resources provide positive environments in which students can thrive. When applied to the classroom setting (as the community), students will excel when they see that their teachers value them. Some of the ways in which teachers can communicate this value to students include engaging them in reciprocal dialogue, involving them in genuine decision-making processes, and getting to know them on a personal level. Students also thrive when they feel they have a role to play in the classroom. As such, teachers can use students as resources in the classroom setting. For example, teachers can identify activities that student leaders can facilitate.

A safe environment with clear boundaries and expectations for students will foster a positive classroom, culture, and learning. As mentioned in chapter 1, all students have the right to feel safe at school, and it is the role of adults in the school setting to ensure that safety is a priority. Similarly, students will be better able to learn and thrive in classrooms in which there are clear rules that delineate the behavioral expectations and boundaries.

How Classroom Management Affects Bullying Behaviors

Important behaviors that teachers can engage in to support classroom management include effective teaching, monitoring, intervention, and personal caring for students. Researchers have found that classrooms in which teachers effectively manage behavior have fewer instances of bullying than classrooms with less effective management.[3]

As all educators know, teachers and school staff have a responsibility to supervise the activities of their students while they are on school grounds. All schools should have policies and procedures in place that promote the effective supervision of students, both during structured time (such as in the classroom) and unstructured time (such as while students walk to and from classes). For more information about how to develop and implement schoolwide policies and procedures that can effectively reduce bullying, please refer to chapter 8.

Researchers have found that teachers view bullying behavior among boys as more normal behavior compared to that of girls.[4] As a result, teachers are more likely to advocate for coping strategies among boys while intervening to stop bullying among girls. It is very important that teachers intervene in all known cases of abusive behavior regardless of the gender of the students.

When students do not feel cared for by their teachers, they are more likely to suffer the consequences of bullying in silence. Students who are bullied and who do not feel supported by their teachers may feel hopeless and helpless to change their situation. Unfortunately, this will support the continued cycle of abuse.

One of the most important things that a teacher can do regarding bullying is to take it seriously. Students cite "teachers not doing anything to help" as one of the biggest reasons why they do not tell an adult at school about bullying. Students who have tried to engage teachers and other school staff to stop bullying but have been ignored are unlikely to go to teachers when future bullying events occur. This can lead to a school culture and climate in which students feel that they have nowhere to turn for help. When that occurs, one of two things typically happens: (1) students become hopeless and helpless to make their situation better (that is, learned helplessness), or (2) students take matters into their own hands through physical aggression or self-harm. Neither of these situations is desirable and both can have very adverse consequences for everyone involved.

Teachers should never ignore a bullying situation but rather should engage all the students who are involved. Students who are being bullied should receive support and help to ensure that their abuse stops and that they are not suffering any adverse consequences, including retaliation. Students who are engaging in bullying behaviors should receive consequences for their behavior and be encouraged to behave in a more prosocial and positive manner (and should be recognized for doing so). Students who witness bullying should be encouraged to step in and try to stop it (whether by allying themselves with the students who are being bullied or finding an adult who can help). More information about how to support each of these student groups can be found in chapter 2 (for students who are bullied), chapter 3 (for students who are bullying), and chapter 4 (for witnesses of bullying).

The Role of Classroom Rules

Chapter 2 describes establishing classroom rules or a student pledge against bullying. These rules and pledges help students explicitly understand that bullying behaviors will not be tolerated and provide them with guidance about the types of prosocial behaviors they should be engaging in while at school and in their classrooms. As mentioned above, clear boundaries and expectations for student behavior facilitate a positive culture and climate. Clear and understandable classroom rules that are consistently enforced can be a very effective tool for providing those boundaries and expectations.

Reinforcement for Prosocial, Positive Behaviors

One of the most commonly neglected behavior management techniques is the use of positive reinforcement to encourage the continuation of behaviors that are positive, prosocial, helpful, caring, and welcome. In some cases, these types of behaviors are not reinforced because people may feel that behaving in a positive way is expected. In other cases, positive behaviors are not reinforced because those who witness them have had little experience with their own positive behavior being reinforced. Whatever the reason, it is important to think about how you as a teacher offer students positive reinforcement for engaging in the types of behaviors that you value.

The first step in providing reinforcement for positive, prosocial behaviors is to define the behavior that you would like to see continue. For example:

- Students waiting quietly in line.

- Students raising their hands to speak.

- Students helping other students pick up something that was dropped.

- Students turning in their schoolwork on time.

These are all examples of behaviors that a teacher may wish to reinforce. It is important for the reinforcement to be given immediately (as soon after the behavior as possible) and enthusiastically. Describe the specific behavior that you are reinforcing while maintaining direct eye contact with the student. The student should feel that the positive reinforcement is sincere and personal. The chart on page 92 lists of many different types of reinforcements for positive student behaviors.

Some forms of reinforcement may not be appropriate in all situations. For example, edible reinforcers are often avoided if there are concerns about nutrition and obesity among students. Similarly, material reinforcers may be cost prohibitive for many teachers. Teachers should select reinforcers that are relevant and meaningful to their students, that fit within the values and policies of the school, and that are sustainable in the long term.

Consequences for Disruptive, Problematic Behaviors

In his book *Schools Where Everyone Belongs: Practical Strategies for Reducing Bullying* (Research Press, 2007), Stan Davis discusses the use of disciplinary rubrics for bullying behavior. In most cases, schools' disciplinary procedures should include consequences for bullying behavior. Effective disciplinary rubrics typically have an escalating series of consequences. Two sample rubrics are included on pages 93–95.

Notes

1. B. Tableman (2004), "School climate and learning: Best practice brief," East Lansing: Michigan State University, University-Community Partnerships.
2. C. S. Anderson (1982), "The search for school climate: A review of the research," *Review of Educational Research, 52,* 368–420; J. P. Comer (1981), *Societal change: Implications for school management,* Washington, DC: National Institute of Education; N. M. Haynes, C. Emmons, & M. Ben-Avie (1997),

"School climate as a factor in student adjustment and achievement," *Journal of Educational and Psychological Consultation, 8,* 321–329; D. Olweus (1994), "Bullying at school: Long-term outcomes for the victims and an effective school-based intervention program," in L. R. Huesmann (Ed.), *Aggressive behavior: Current perspectives* (97–130), New York: Plenum; D. Olweus & S. Limber (2002), *Blueprints for violence prevention: Bullying prevention program,* Boulder: University of Colorado, Institute of Behavioral Science; M. Rutter, N. Maughan, P. Mortimore, J. Ouston, & A. Smith (1979), *Fifteen thousand hours: Secondary schools and their effects on children,* Cambridge, MA: Harvard University Press; Wingspread Conference (2004), "Wingspread declaration on school connections," *Journal of School Health, 74,* 233–234.

3. J. Drake (2003), "Teacher preparation and practices regarding school bullying," *Journal of School Health,* 347–356; B. Kochenderfer-Ladd & M.E. Pelletier (2008), "Teachers' views and beliefs about bullying: Influences on classroom management strategies and students' coping with peer victimization," *Journal of School Psychology*, *46,* 431–453; E. Roland & D. Galloway (2002), "Classroom influences on bullying," *Educational Research*, *44*(3), 299–312.

4. B. Kochenderfer-Ladd & M.E. Pelletier (2008), "Teachers' views and beliefs about bullying: Influences on classroom management strategies and students' coping with peer victimization," *Journal of School Psychology*, *46,* 431–453.

5. Valley Park Elementary, 12301 Lamar Ave., Overland Park, KS 66209.

6. East Middle School, 2600 Grand Ave., Butte, MT 59701.

REINFORCERS FOR POSITIVE STUDENT BEHAVIORS

Sensory Reinforcers	Physical Reinforcers	Edible Reinforcers
• Listening to music on an MP3 player • Choosing a poster • Viewing a kaleidoscope • Smelling soaps • Sitting in a rocking chair • Playing a CD • Selecting a perfume • Blowing party noisemakers • Petting a stuffed animal • Rubbing on a hand lotion • Using a back scratcher • Collecting glow-in-the-dark bugs • Burning incense • Tossing balloons • Seeing cartoons on a viewfinder • Blowing bubbles	• Playing a game • Erasing the blackboard • Being a team captain • Putting up a bulletin board • Free time with a friend • Operating equipment • Shooting baskets • Being an office assistant • Sitting next to a friend • Handing out calculators	• Bananas • Cookies • Cereal • Cubes of Jell-O • Raisins • Candy • Pudding • Soda • Juice
Material Reinforcers	**Token Reinforcers**	**Social Reinforcers**
• Stickers • CDs • Pencils • Plastic ants • Bookmarks • Wax teeth • Erasers • A hand buzzer • Trading cards • Disappearing ink • Movie tickets • Magic tricks • Food coupons • Masks • Clay • Candy or gum • Cassette tapes	• Raffle tickets • Tokens • Poker chips • Points • Credits	• A smile • A wink • A nice compliment • Effective praise

EXAMPLE OF ELEMENTARY SCHOOL DISCIPLINARY RUBRIC FOR BULLYING (FROM VALLEY PARK ELEMENTARY)[5]

Behavior	FIRST INCIDENT	SECOND INCIDENT RETALIATION	THIRD INCIDENT RETALIATION	FOURTH INCIDENT RETALIATION
Calling a student a mean name, making fun of a student, teasing a student in a hurtful, intimidating way	• Verbal behavior reminder • Discipline referral, written warning • Letter to parent(s) that must be signed and returned	• Privilege loss (two days) • Discipline referral • Student calls parent(s) to report incident • Letter to parent(s) that must be signed and returned • Reflection sheet	• Classes only (three days) • Discipline referral • Student calls parent(s) to report incident • Letter to parent(s) that must be signed and returned • Reflection sheet • Meet with counselor	• Discipline referral • Meet with principal • Meet with school staff to coordinate individual plan • Consequences determined by administrator
Socially excluding a student on purpose, ignoring a student to be hurtful, encouraging others not to like someone	• Verbal behavior reminder • Discipline referral, written warning • Letter to parent(s) that must be signed and returned	• Privilege loss (two days) • Discipline referral • Student calls parent(s) to report incident • Letter to parent(s) that must be signed and returned • Reflection sheet	• Classes only (three days) • Discipline referral • Student calls parent(s) to report incident • Letter to parent(s) that must be signed and returned • Reflection sheet • Meet with counselor	• Discipline referral • Meet with principal • Meet with school staff to coordinate individual plan • Consequences determined by administrator
Spreading rumors or telling lies to encourage others to dislike another student	• Verbal behavior reminder • Discipline referral, written warning • Letter to parent(s) that must be signed and returned	• Privilege loss (two days) • Discipline referral • Student calls parent(s) to report incident • Letter to parent(s) that must be signed and returned • Reflection sheet	• Classes only (three days) • Discipline referral • Student calls parent(s) to report incident • Letter to parent(s) that must be signed and returned • Reflection sheet • Meet with counselor	• Discipline referral • Meet with principal • Meet with school staff to coordinate individual plan • Consequences determined by administrator
Engaging in inappropriate but not aggressive or unsafe actions (rough play/ messing around)	• Verbal behavior reminder • Discipline referral, written warning • Letter to parent(s) that must be signed and returned	• Privilege loss (two days) • Discipline referral • Student calls parent(s) to report incident • Letter to parent(s) that must be signed and returned • Reflection sheet	• Classes only (three days) • Discipline referral • Student calls parent(s) to report incident • Letter to parent(s) that must be signed and returned • Reflection sheet • Meet with counselor	• Discipline referral • Meet with principal • Meet with school staff to coordinate individual plan • Consequences determined by administrator

continued ➡

EXAMPLE OF ELEMENTARY SCHOOL DISCIPLINARY RUBRIC FOR BULLYING (FROM VALLEY PARK ELEMENTARY)[5]

Behavior	FIRST INCIDENT	SECOND INCIDENT RETALIATION	THIRD INCIDENT RETALIATION	FOURTH INCIDENT RETALIATION
Displaying aggressive actions toward another student (bumping, kicking, pushing, shoving, biting, spitting, choking, pulling hair), making threats	• Privilege loss (two days) • Discipline referral • Student calls parent(s) to report incident • Letter to parent(s) that must be signed and returned • Reflection sheet	• Classes only (three days) • Discipline referral • Student calls parent(s) to report incident • Letter to parent(s) that must be signed and returned • Reflection sheet • Meet with counselor	• Discipline referral • Meet with principal • Meet with school staff to coordinate individual plan • Consequences determined by administrator	• Office referral • Consequences determined by administrator
Harassment (racial, ethnic, or sexual name-calling or severe harassment): verbal, written, or via media including but not limited to text messaging, e-mail, or web postings. This may include inappropriate postings, spreading rumors, or posting inappropriate pictures	• Privilege loss (two days) • Discipline referral • Student calls parent(s) to report incident • Letter to parent(s) that must be signed and returned • Reflection sheet	• Classes only (three days) • Discipline referral • Student calls parent(s) to report incident • Letter to parent(s) that must be signed and returned • Reflection sheet • Meet with counselor	• Discipline referral • Meet with principal • Meet with school staff to coordinate individual plan • Consequences determined by administrator	• Office referral • Consequences determined by administrator
Exposing oneself or others by lifting clothing or "pantsing"; making rude, inappropriate comments or gestures	• Administration will determine consequences.			
Fighting **Severe behavior: putting oneself or others at risk, continued or severe aggression, threat of severe aggression** **Bringing inappropriate objects to school (such as weapons)**	• Referral to administration. Administration will determine consequences. Pursuant to K.S.A. 72-89b03 and district policy. If the student has broken the law, the principal must notify law enforcement.			

EXAMPLE OF MIDDLE SCHOOL DISCIPLINARY RUBRIC (FROM EAST MIDDLE SCHOOL)[6]

VERBAL BULLYING BEHAVIOR	NONVERBAL BULLYING BEHAVIOR	PHYSICAL BULLYING BEHAVIOR	*Consequence menu*
• Passing notes • Gossiping • Starting/spreading rumors • Teasing about possessions (clothes, looks, etc.) • False reporting • Name-calling • Insulting remarks • Making threats	• Threatening or insulting gestures • Dirty looks • Ignoring or excluding others • Hiding items from others • Writing/passing notes	• Pushing, shoving, poking • In other people's space • Blocking other people's path • Intimidation (in the hallway or classroom)	• *Phone call home* • *Reminder/warning* • *Think sheet* • *Team consequences* • *Reteach expectations* • *Counseling referral* • *Team-parent meeting* • *Detention*
• Prolonged harassment • Encouraging total group exclusion of someone by threatening others if they don't comply • Sexual harassment • Chronic level 2 behaviors	• Destroying property • Setting fires • Arranging public humiliation • Writing graffiti of any kind • Chronic level 2 behaviors	• Spitting on others • Biting others • Making repeated or graphic threats • Extortion • Threatening to keep someone silent • Physical harm • Acts of violence • Assault • Chronic level 2 behaviors	• *Phone call home* • *Disciplinary referral* • *Counseling referral* • *In-school suspension* • *Out-of-school suspension* • *Restitution* • *Law enforcement referral* • *Parent meeting* • *Referral to superintendent's office* • *Expulsion referral*

CHAPTER 7

Partnering with Parents to Stop Bullying

A positive parent-teacher relationship helps your child feel good about school and be successful in school. . . . This positive relationship makes a child feel like the important people in his life are working together.

—DR. DIANE LEVIN, PROFESSOR OF EDUCATION

As you will recall from chapter 2, approximately 17 percent of students experience bullying. This includes both students who are bullied and students who are bullied *and* bully others. We know that some of these students will disclose their bullying to their parents/guardians. When a child discloses that he is being bullied at school, parents/guardians often struggle with how they should react.

Teachers often wonder, "Why are parents/guardians so hesitant to approach school officials when their child is being bullied?" The following are some of the reasons for this hesitation.

Many parents/guardians believe that they may make bullying situations worse for their children if they involve adults at school. They may fear that by involving the school, their child will be singled out among peers, which can lead to more abuse. This is a legitimate fear in cases where students may receive special support or attention from school officials, such as escorts to class. Sometimes, parents/guardians do not contact the school because their child fears retaliation, embarrassment, or being singled out. This causes them to beg their parents/guardians not to contact the school. Similarly, parents/guardians may also be embarrassed that their child is being bullied and are uncomfortable sharing their family's vulnerability with school officials.

In other cases, parents/guardians are unsure how best to help their children when they are bullied. Many people who are unsure what to do in a situation tend to do nothing. Parents/guardians of children who are bullied are no different, especially if they feel that bullying that occurs in the school setting is outside their realm of control. Unfortunately, in some cases, parents/guardians have approached school officials but have been told that there is nothing that can be done. This leads to a sense of powerlessness.

Other parents/guardians do nothing because they believe they will be seen as overprotective if they intervene in a problematic situation with their child's peers. This may stem from a belief that it is their child's responsibility to handle the bullying situation. In this case, parents/guardians are unaware that bullying is an abusive situation in which their child's peers have more power and control than their child.

Teachers and school officials can help parents/guardians understand the impact of bullying, including specific and effective ways in which they can help. Children need people at home *and* people at school who can help them stop bullying. Parents/guardians should be encouraged to report instances of bullying to the school, and school officials should be expected to do everything in their power to stop the bullying. As we emphasized in chapter 1, everyone has a right to feel safe and secure at school and no one should have to tolerate abuse.

F.A.Q.

Teachers often wonder, "Why are parents/guardians so hesitant to approach school officials when their child is being bullied?" Parents may hesitate because:

- They fear making a bullying situation worse.
- Their bullied child asks them not to.
- They are unsure what to do.
- They feel powerless.
- They are embarrassed.
- They fear being overprotective and/or believe it's the child's responsibility to handle the bullying.

PARENTS/GUARDIANS OF STUDENTS WHO BULLY OTHERS

As you will recall from chapter 2, approximately 19 percent of students engage in bullying behaviors toward their peers. This includes both students who bully others and students who bully others *and* are bullied themselves. The parents/guardians of these students should be notified when their child is behaving in an abusive way toward other students. This type of news can be very difficult for a parent/guardian to hear. The following are some things to take into consideration when talking with the parent(s)/guardian(s) of a student who is bullying.

Bullying is a behavior: It is the child's behavior that is problematic in cases of bullying. Too often, students are called *bullies* rather than *students who are engaging in bullying behavior*. It is essential to avoid categorizing these students as bullies because that assumes that bullying is a permanent characteristic when in fact it is a problematic behavior that can be altered with the right awareness, consequences, support, and supervision. Please refer to chapter 1's "Bullying Is a Behavior" section for a more detailed discussion about this.

There are always multiple sides to any story: In many cases, students who bully others will explain why they bully to their parents/guardians. They may articulate that the other student did something to them that caused them to react in a bullying manner. Regardless of what the student perceives as the impetus, it is important to focus on the child's behavior (and her responsibility for her behavior). Engaging in bullying behavior is wrong no matter what. It is important to keep the conversation focused on the child's behavior rather than on the other student's actions or deficits.

Proviolent attitudes and beliefs: In some families, using violence to solve problems can be the norm. In these cases, it can be difficult for a teacher to discuss a student's bullying behavior with the child's parent(s)/guardian(s) because they may approve of and condone such behavior. When this occurs, teachers and other school staff should work to identify ways in which the child's aggressive behavior can be funneled into positive situations. For example, many students who bully have natural leadership characteristics. These leadership qualities should be cultivated through activities that help, rather than harm, the larger peer group.

THE ROLE OF TEACHERS AND OTHER ADULTS AT SCHOOL

There are a variety of things that teachers and other adults at school can do when they have identified bullying situations. Teachers should ensure that all of their students' parents/guardians receive copies of the school's anti-bullying policies and procedures. Please refer to chapter 8 for more information about developing schoolwide policies and procedures to address bullying behaviors. By ensuring that all parents/guardians are aware of the school's role in bullying, they will have a better understanding of how the school can help their children.

Hopefully, the school's policies and procedures will include a mechanism for school staff to immediately investigate instances of bullying. Someone at the school should meet with students who are being bullied to find out what the students have experienced. A safety plan should be developed to help keep the students who were bullied safe from future harm. All staff members who know the students should be informed of the abuse so they can assist in keeping a watchful eye on the students. Responsible adults at school should assure both the students and the students' parents/guardians that they will work hard to keep the students safe and secure so they can focus on learning and succeeding at school.

It is very important for teachers and parents/guardians to avoid blaming the student who is bullied for what has happened to her. Children who are abused are not responsible for their abuse and should not be expected to stop the bullying from occurring. Please see chapter 1 for an additional discussion about this. In cases in which students who are bullied experience social, emotional, or behavioral consequences as a result of their abuse, they should be encouraged to talk with a school counselor.

Someone at the school should also meet with the student who is suspected of taking part in the bullying. The student should be reminded that bullying is against school rules and will not be tolerated. If the bullying accusation is substantiated, the school's disciplinary procedures should be followed and students who are bullying others should receive consequences. School officials should inform the parents/guardians of the students who are involved what they plan to do about the bullying behaviors.

Next, a thorough investigation of the bullying should take place. It is helpful to talk with everyone who may have information about the situation, including any witnesses to the abuse. Although a thorough investigation is critical, it should be conducted in a timely manner. It is essential to understand what is occurring as quickly as possible and to take actions to keep students safe and secure from future harm and abuse.

Conflict resolution strategies or mediation meetings between the two parties should never occur when a student is being bullied. Remember that bullying is a form of peer abuse and is not a conflict or disagreement between two equal peers. For more information about what is and is not bullying, please refer to chapter 1.

After students have been identified as being involved in bullying, regular supervision and follow-up may be needed. Parents/guardians should be encouraged to keep records of additional bullying concerns and share those with school officials. Parents/guardians should understand whom to go to for help with bullying. If they do not receive satisfactory assistance from these people, they should be made aware of additional people (such as administrators and superintendents) who can help.

Parents/guardians should be informed about the various roles that teachers and other school staff members can play in reducing and/or preventing bullying. It is essential, however, for teachers to understand that the child's parent(s)/guardian(s) are the expert on the child and his behavior. As such, parents/guardians should be considered essential allies when working to reduce and/or prevent bullying behaviors. The following section describes ways in which to partner with a student's parent(s)/guardian(s) when he has been involved in bullying.

PARTNERING WITH PARENTS/GUARDIANS

Phone Calls: Calling Parents/Guardians

About Students Who Bully: When a student has been identified as bullying other peers, the student's parent(s)/guardian(s) should be notified and the following topics should be discussed:

1. The specific behavior(s) that the student displayed.

2. The school's rules against the identified behavior(s).

3. The consequences that the student will receive as a result of the behavior.

4. Additional information that the parent(s)/guardian(s) may have regarding the child's behavior.

5. Suggestions that the parent(s)/guardian(s) may have regarding appropriate discipline for their child.

6. Specific ways in which the parent(s)/guardian(s) can support the school's discipline of the student.

7. Concrete, tangible suggestions for how the student should behave in the future.

The school's policies about confidentiality should be followed with regard to naming the other students who were involved. This consideration should be outlined in the school's anti-bullying policies and procedures. Please refer to chapter 8 for suggestions about including parental/guardian notification procedures in the school's anti-bullying policies.

About Students Who Are Bullied: When a student has been identified as being bullied by other peers, the student's parent(s)/guardian(s) should be notified and the following topics should be discussed:

1. The specific ways in which the student has been bullied.

2. The school's rules against the identified behavior(s).

3. The consequences that the other student will receive as a result of her behavior.

4. Additional information that the parent(s)/guardian(s) may have regarding any other abuse the child may have experienced.

5. Suggestions that the parent(s)/guardian(s) may have regarding appropriate ways to keep their child safe from future harm.

6. The specific ways in which the school will keep the student who has been bullied safe from future abuse.

7. Specific ways in which the parent(s)/guardian(s) can support the school in keeping their child safe.

Parents/guardians should be provided with concrete, tangible solutions that the school will implement to keep any additional abusive behavior from occurring. If the student who was bullied has lasting emotional symptoms related to the abuse, the school can provide the family with a referral to a mental health specialist who can support the child's emotional healing. Parents/guardians should be encouraged to contact the school if their child discloses any additional information to them about being bullied again.

About Students Who Witness Bullying: In some cases, it may be valuable to inform parents/guardians that their child has witnessed bullying (and perhaps joined in or stepped in to stop the bullying). The goal of these conversations should be to elicit their assistance in reinforcing positive values and behaviors in their children. If the child joined in the bullying, the parents/guardians can discuss the reasons why that behavior is unacceptable with their child. If the child stepped in to stop the bullying, they can congratulate their child on a job well done.

Follow-up Letters: Writing to Parents and Guardians

About Students Who Bully: After the initial notification about a specific event, it is helpful to connect with parents/guardians at some point in the future to discuss whether or not their child has made appropriate behavioral changes. School staff can share information with parents/guardians about any additional behavioral/disciplinary referrals that the child has received. Following up with parents/guardians will let them know that the school takes abusive behavior very seriously and that they want the involvement and help of the student's parent(s)/guardian(s) over the long term. Parents/guardians can be instrumental in supporting the school's disciplinary consequences for their child.

About Students Who Are Bullied: Students who experience bullying can experience a wide range of social, emotional, behavioral, and academic consequences as a result of being abused. Many of these can be lasting, and it is important to contact the parent(s)/guardian(s) of the student who was bullied to let them know how the student has been coping at school. It is reassuring to parents/guardians to know that the school cares enough about their children's safety and well-being to regularly check in and follow up on how things are progressing. Parent(s)/guardian(s) should be encouraged to share any additional concerns that they have about their children's experience of bullying, and they should expect that someone at the school will be responsive and helpful regarding those concerns.

About Students Who Witness Bullying: In some cases, school staff may want to follow up with the parents/guardians of students who witnessed a bullying situation. For those who joined in the bullying, it is important to inform the parents/guardians about whether or not improvement has been made in their child's behavior. Parents/guardians can continue to reinforce better values and behavior in their children at home. For students who stepped in to stop the bullying, school staff may wish to share additional positive behaviors that the child has displayed. It is very positive for parents/guardians to hear that their child is behaving in a way that is celebrated by the school.

The handout on the next page provides a sample letter to the parents/guardians of students involved in bullying.

Face-to-Face Meetings: Talking with Parents/Guardians

About Students Who Bully: If bullying behavior continues to be a problem, school officials may wish to meet with parents/guardians face-to-face. This meeting should be used as a problem-solving meeting in which everyone can partner together to develop solutions to the child's continued abusive behavior. Solutions should be strength-based whenever possible. When all other options have been tried, suspension and expulsion may be used.

About Students Who Are Bullied: If a student continues to be abused by his peers, school officials may wish to meet with the student's parent(s)/guardian(s) face-to-face. This meeting should be used to develop an intensive safety plan for the student. Identify specific school staff who can remain vigilant throughout the day and ensure that the safety plan is implemented. A safety plan should outline what the student needs to feel safe, what the student should do if the bullying continues, and whom the student should tell if he is bullied again.

About Students Who Witness Bullying: In some cases, it may be important to invite the parents/guardians of students who have witnessed bullying behavior to meet with school officials. As with the parents/guardians of students who bully others, the parents/guardians of bystander students who joined in the bullying should work with school officials to develop solutions to their children's problematic behavior. If initial attempts to change the behavior are unsuccessful, a face-to-face meeting can be called to problem-solve and develop appropriate consequences and/or solutions to the students' behavior.

Sample Letter to Parents/Guardians
of Students Involved in Bullying

[Today's Date]

[Name of Parent/Guardian]
[Address]
[City, State, ZIP]

Dear [Parent's/Guardian's name],
[In this paragraph, say who you are and the nature of your relationship to the student.]

[Briefly explain why you are writing. Give relevant history and facts that support your concerns. (For example, the student is being bullied/is bullying in school and you want to ask the parent/guardian for help. Talk about relevant facts such as your concerns about the student's behavior, grades, peer relationships, etc.)]

[In this paragraph, state what you would like to have happen or what you would like to see changed. Discuss what the school's policies and procedures are regarding bullying. Discuss how the student will be affected by those policies and procedures. Identify what the school will do to keep the student safe or to discipline the student, and identify what the parent/guardian can do to help.]

[Finally, give your daytime telephone number and state that you look forward to hearing from the parent/guardian soon or give a date. ("Please respond by the 15th.")]

Thank you for your attention to this matter.

Sincerely,
[Your name]
[Your title]
[Your contact information]

This handout may be reproduced for educational, noncommercial uses only (with this copyright line). From *The Right to Be Safe: Putting an End to Bullying Behavior* by Cricket Meehan, Ph.D. Copyright © 2011 Search Institute®, Minneapolis, MN; 877-240-7251 ext. 1; www.search-institute.org. All rights reserved.

Sample Agenda for Meeting with the Parents/Guardians of Students Involved in Bullying

1. Introduce everyone attending the meeting and identify each person's role.

2. Discuss the bullying behaviors that have occurred (please follow the school's confidentiality procedures regarding identifying other students' names).

   • For students who have bullied other students, identify what types of discipline have been used and how effective the discipline has been.

   • For students who have been bullied, discuss the impact of the bullying on the student and what type of safety procedures have been implemented. Talk about how effective those safety procedures have been.

3. Determine what needs to happen to ensure that bullying does not happen again in the future.

   • For students who have bullied others, identify several options for relevant and meaningful discipline or punishment. Whenever possible, identify strengths within the student that can be reinforced to help her make better decisions. Get everyone's input on which option should be selected.

   • For students who have been bullied, develop an intensive safety plan to ensure that the student can attend school safely and securely. Priority should be given to ensure that the student feels that she can concentrate and focus on learning rather than worrying about being bullied.

4. Identify how the above-mentioned solutions will be implemented, and select a time frame in which to provide regular updates to everyone in attendance at the meeting about progress that has been made.

5. Hold everyone accountable for doing his part to stop the bullying from happening again.

This handout may be reproduced for educational, noncommercial uses only (with this copyright line). From *The Right to Be Safe: Putting an End to Bullying Behavior* by Cricket Meehan, Ph.D. Copyright © 2011 Search Institute®, Minneapolis, MN; 877-240-7251 ext. 1; www.search-institute.org. All rights reserved.

PARTNERING WITH PARENTS/GUARDIANS ON ANTI-BULLYING EFFORTS

Raising Awareness of Classroom Anti-Bullying Lessons/Discussions

Most parents/guardians welcome the opportunity to help their children learn. When teachers send home updates about what children are learning in the classrooms, parents/guardians feel empowered to support their children. When they hear a similar message both at school and at home, children tend to recognize the importance of the message. After discussing anti-bullying-related topics with students in the classroom, teachers should send home a brief outline of the topics covered, along with a set of activities and questions that parents/guardians can use at home to further the discussion.

Recall from chapter 4 that several important anti-bullying-related classroom discussion topics were introduced. One of those topics, *telling versus tattling/snitching,* should be discussed early with students. Parents/guardians should also be provided with the same key concepts (see the handout on page 106):

- Telling is done to keep the person who is being bullied safe.

- It is expected that the person who is confided in has the ability to step in and stop the bullying from happening.

- Tattling/snitching is done to get someone who has acted in an inappropriate way in trouble.

- Some students do not tell an adult about bullying because they fear that the student who is bullying may retaliate against them if he or she finds out who told.

- In other cases, students may not tell because they do not believe that the adult will do anything effective to stop the bullying.

Some questions that teachers can provide parents/guardians with include:

- Do you feel safe at school?

- Do you have an adult at school whom you can talk to if you are having a problem?

- What sorts of things can you do if you know that one of your friends is being bullied?

- What happens to people at school who tell on a student who is behaving badly?

Teachers can send home similar key concepts and discussion questions for each of the various classroom discussions they hold with their students. Students can be encouraged to help their teachers create these informational forms so parents/guardians are receiving information that is truly relevant and meaningful to their children.

Sample Informational Sheet
for Parents/Guardians
on the Classroom Meeting Topic
Telling versus Tattling/Snitching

Key concepts that parents/guardians should be aware of:

- Telling is done to keep the person who is being bullied safe.

- It is expected that the person who is confided in has the ability to step in and stop the bullying from happening.

- Tattling/snitching is done to get someone who has acted in an inappropriate way in trouble.

- Some students do not tell an adult about bullying because they fear that the student who is bullying may retaliate against them if he or she finds out who told.

- In other cases, students may not tell because they do not believe that the adult will do anything effective to stop the bullying.

Questions that parents/guardians can discuss with their children:

- Do you feel safe at school?

- Do you have an adult at school whom you can talk to if you are having a problem?

- What sorts of things can you do if you know that one of your friends is being bullied?

- What happens to people at school who tell on a student who is behaving badly?

This handout may be reproduced for educational, noncommercial uses only (with this copyright line). From *The Right to Be Safe: Putting an End to Bullying Behavior* by Cricket Meehan, Ph.D. Copyright © 2011 Search Institute®, Minneapolis, MN; 877-240-7251 ext. 1; www.search-institute.org. All rights reserved.

HELPING PARENTS/GUARDIANS TALK WITH THEIR CHILDREN ABOUT BULLYING AT HOME

When encouraging parents/guardians to talk with their children about bullying, it can be helpful to provide them with some basic information about bullying. For example, remind them that bullying is a behavior and behaviors can be modified and changed. Parents/guardians should be encouraged to talk with their children about any experiences with bullying that they may have. Parents/guardians can keep written documentation of these events, which can be shared with a caring adult at the school. They should document the who, what, where, and when of the bullying situation.

When bullying has been identified, parents/guardians and teachers should set up a meeting to develop safety plans for the students who are being bullied and disciplinary plans for the students who are engaging in the bullying. This should be a partnership between parents/guardians and teachers with the common goal of keeping students safe and stopping any problematic behavior from occurring again. For students who are experiencing social, emotional, behavioral, or academic disturbances, parents/guardians and teachers can decide if a referral to the school counselor or a mental health professional is warranted. Following the meeting, parents/guardians and teachers should remain in regular contact to determine if the situation has improved over the long term or if additional intervention is needed.

There are several resources that teachers can share with parents/guardians of students who are being bullied. These resources will help parents/guardians talk with their children about bullying experiences. If bullying or cyberbullying is occurring, the U.S. Health Resources and Services Administration lists a number of steps that parents/guardians can take to help prevent and/or respond to it at stopbullying.gov/parents/index.html. The Centers for Disease Control has information about electronic aggression available for parents/guardians at cdc.gov/ViolencePrevention/youthviolence/electronicaggression/index.html.

Ideas Parents/Guardians Can Use to Reinforce Knowledge and Skills at Home

In general, the positive values, attitudes, and beliefs that parents/guardians have about what it means to be a good person can provide the foundation for reinforcing knowledge and skills at home. Parents/guardians can engage their children in conversations about the values that are important to their family. In addition, parents/guardians should be encouraged to identify the strengths that their children possess and help their children see how they can use those strengths to stand up to bullying and have positive relationships with their peers.

Providing School Policies and Procedures to Parents/Guardians

All parents/guardians should be provided with copies of the school's anti-bullying policies and procedures. Parents/guardians should be provided with the opportunity to review the documents and ask any questions that they may have about them. When cases of bullying occur, parents/guardians of the involved students should be reminded of the school's policies and procedures. School officials should inform them of exactly how their child will be disciplined (in the case of bullying) or protected and kept safe (in the case of being bullied).

It can also be helpful to provide parents/guardians with the opportunity to critique the policies and procedures and offer suggestions to improve them. Typically, policies that have broad representation from all the parties who are affected by them will prove to be the most useful and effective. In addition, this creates a sense among parents/guardians that the school is truly willing to partner with them in the quest to reduce and prevent bullying at the school.

An Update to Ben's Story

Too often, partnerships between parents and teachers do not occur. This is what happened in Ben's case. Ben's parents repeatedly approached school officials with their concerns about Ben's abuse. When that did not work, they wrote a letter to officials in the district. Unfortunately, they still did not receive satisfactory support. As a result of getting no resolution to the bullying problems, Ben's parents pulled him from his original school and placed him in a new school.

Luckily for him, Ben is thriving at his new school. He is making As and Bs in all his classes, which is quite a change from the grades he was receiving at his old school. He joined several extracurricular activities and has made many new friends. He attends the school's football games every week and even had a date to the homecoming dance.

His parents believe that the attitudes and the safety structure at Ben's new school account for much of the success that he has experienced. Ben's mother noted that the teachers and other school staff are really into the kids and accept them for who they are. The school has security cameras that monitor all areas of the school building.

The move is not without hardships for Ben's family, however. Ben's mother had to turn down a promotion at work and change her schedule to evenings and weekends in order to transport Ben to and from his new school and activities. Several nights each week, Ben's mother can only sleep from 3 a.m. to 6 a.m. due to this new schedule. She recognizes, though, that this is the only way she can ensure that her son has an opportunity to learn, participate, and enjoy his high school experience.

CHAPTER 8

Schoolwide Policies and Procedures against Bullying

Ultimately, what we know is that when bullying is addressed, kids will perform better academically.

—DR. DOROTHY ESPELAGE, PROFESSOR OF EDUCATIONAL PSYCHOLOGY

Many states now have guidelines for anti-bullying behaviors in school settings. Appendix C discusses some of the most common features that are included in anti-bullying legislation, including a summary of the current laws in the United States. Below are some general guidelines that districts and schools should consider when adopting anti-bullying policies and procedures.

DEVELOPMENT OF POLICIES AND PROCEDURES

Definition of Bullying

The most important first step in creating policies and procedures to prohibit bullying is to define what bullying is. A definition of bullying will help everyone understand the specific types of behaviors that are included in the anti-bullying policy. Definitions of bullying should be

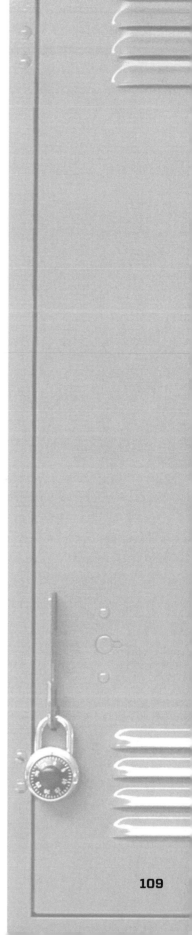

clear, concise, specific, and easily understandable. You may recall the Olweus definition of bullying:

> *A person is bullied when he or she is exposed, repeatedly and over time, to negative actions on the part of one or more other persons, and he or she has difficulty defending himself or herself.*

While this definition helps us understand bullying in an abstract sense, many school districts find it necessary to expand upon this definition. Many states have developed statewide model anti-bullying educational policies. Throughout this chapter, the model policy developed by the State of Ohio's Department of Education (DOE) will be used as an example. Ohio's DOE has developed the following model policy definition to guide its districts in the adoption of policies prohibiting harassment, intimidation, and bullying:

> *Harassment, intimidation, or bullying means any intentional written, verbal, graphic, or physical act that a student or group of students has exhibited toward another student more than once and the behavior both:*
>
> - *Causes mental or physical harm to the other student and*
>
> - *Is sufficiently severe, persistent, or pervasive that it creates an intimidating, threatening, or abusive educational environment for the other student.*

> *Harassment, intimidation, and bullying can also be transmitted electronically, that is, over the Internet or with a cell phone, a personal digital assistant (PDA), or a wireless handheld device. As with physical acts, electronic harassment, intimidation, and bullying are intentional acts that a student or group of students has exhibited toward another particular student more than once and the behavior both:*
>
> - *Causes mental or physical harm to the other student/school personnel and*
>
> - *Is sufficiently severe, persistent, or pervasive that it creates an intimidating, threatening, or abusive educational environment for the other student/school personnel.*

This model policy definition is specific, concise, clear, and understandable. It identifies specific forms that bullying behavior can take. Specific components of bullying are outlined, including abusive behavior that is repeated. It also identifies the consequences that this behavior can have on the students who are targeted.

The Ohio Department of Education's model policy also explicitly identifies the specific behavior for harassment, intimidation, and bullying. According to their model policy:

Harassment, intimidation, or bullying can include many different behaviors, including overt intent to ridicule, humiliate, or intimidate another student or school personnel. Examples of conduct that could constitute prohibited behaviors include:

- *Physical violence and/or attacks*

- *Threats, taunts, and intimidation through words and/or gestures*

- *Extortion, damage, or stealing of money and/or possessions*

- *Exclusion from the peer group or spreading rumors*

- *Repetitive and hostile behavior with the intent to harm others through the use of information and communication technologies and other Web-based/online sites (also known as cyberbullying), such as the following:*

- *Posting slurs on websites where students congregate or on web logs (personal online journals or diaries)*

- *Sending abusive or threatening instant messages*

- *Using camera phones to take embarrassing photographs of students and posting them online*

- *Using websites to circulate gossip and rumors to other students*

- *Excluding others from an online group by falsely reporting them for inappropriate language to Internet service providers.*

The criteria that are included in this model policy provide guidelines for school districts to use to differentiate between bullying, harassment, intimidation, and other forms of aggressive behavior. The criteria outline very specific types of behavior that are considered bullying, harassment, and/or intimidation.

Discipline and Consequences for Bullying Behaviors

Once bullying has been accurately identified, the students who are engaging in the problematic behaviors should receive disciplinary consequences for their abusive behavior. Anti-bullying policies and procedures need to include detailed information for teachers and school staff to follow regarding disciplinary procedures.

 F.A.Q.

"Do schools have the responsibility to address cyberbullying that occurs off campus?" Although this is still a somewhat controversial topic, the current consensus among most experts is that any cyberbullying behavior—whether it occurs at home, at school, or elsewhere—has the potential to cause substantial disruption to the educational environment within the school setting. An example of substantial disruption would include vicious and hurtful rumors and gossiping at school that occur as a result of something posted online. Legal experts believe that schools have a responsibility to take actions to end any reactionary behaviors or bullying that occur as a result of students' awareness of cyberbullying incidents. For more information about this very complex issue, please refer to Nancy E. Willard's book *Cyberbullying and Cyberthreats: Responding to the Challenge of Online Social Aggression, Threats, and Distress* (Research Press, 2007).

Some schools have incorporated disciplinary procedures for bullying into their already existing behavioral disciplinary policies. Other schools have developed a separate set of consequences when students bully others. Regardless of which version your school selects, it is important to keep some key considerations in mind.

First, there are many different forms that bullying can take. It can be physical, verbal, social, direct, indirect, in person, or through technology. Bullying behaviors can also differ in the severity and the length of abuse. Type, length, and severity of bullying behaviors should be considered when determining the most appropriate consequences. For instance, first-time offenses will likely receive more lenient consequences compared to repeat offenses. Each of these factors should be taken into consideration when developing a disciplinary procedure for bullying behaviors. Examples of disciplinary rubrics for elementary and middle schools can be found in chapter 6.

The consequences that are selected should be relevant and meaningful to your student body. The goal of a negative consequence is to deter bullying from occurring again. If students receive consequences that are not sufficiently adverse, the likelihood that they will stop bullying in the future is greatly diminished. Individual students will also react to specific consequences differently. As such, it is important to have a variety of disciplinary choices at your disposal.

When a student has received disciplinary consequences for bullying behavior, the student's parent(s)/guardian(s) should be notified. It is beneficial to include procedures for notifying parents/guardians in the school's anti-bullying policy. In some cases, the principal or assistant principal may be the person responsible for talking with parents/guardians. In other cases, a school may prefer to have the teacher, school counselor, or behavior specialist notify the parents/guardians. To ensure timely notification, it is encouraged that schools outline the time frame in which parents/guardians will be contacted within the school's anti-bullying policy.

Positive Reinforcement for Prosocial Behavior

In addition to using disciplinary action to reduce problematic behaviors, it is important to provide positive reinforcement for students who engage in positive, prosocial, helpful behaviors. The goal of positive reinforcement is to strengthen the positive behavior so the likelihood that students will repeat similar behavior in the future is greatly augmented. Students who see one of their peers being recognized for good behavior may also be more likely to engage in similar behavior in the future.

While it is important to contact the parents/guardians of students who bully, it is equally important to contact the parents/guardians of students who engage in prosocial behavior. Too often, schools only contact parents/guardians when there is a problem. By sharing the news that a child has been recognized for good behavior, teachers enlist parents/guardians in reinforcing these prosocial values at home and help them feel a sense of pride in their children. Issues of confidentiality regarding identifying the other students who were involved should be considered based on the school's confidentiality policy.

Dissemination of the School District's Anti-Bullying Policy

Once a policy has been established at the district or school level, it is essential that everyone is aware of the specific policies and procedures. All school staff, students, and students' parents/guardians should receive copies of and/or access to the anti-bullying policy. Teachers and other school staff would benefit from professional development training opportunities that explain the policy and delineate their specific roles in carrying it out. Students and their families should be given ample opportunities to review the policy and ask any questions they may have regarding its implementation.

Working with Administrators and Boards

In some cases, teachers and other school staff members may be in a position to assist their school's administration and boards in the development of an anti-bullying policy. Teachers can encourage their administrators to consider developing and adopting an anti-bullying policy if one does not already exist. Teachers can share the types of behaviors that they witness within their classrooms and the school setting in order to provide administrators and boards with knowledge about what is happening at the school. Many states now mandate that schools have policies in place (please see appendix C for a complete list of those states).

DISCIPLINARY/SUPERVISORY SYSTEMS

The school's anti-bullying policy should include specific steps to take when consequences are deserved. In addition, the policy should outline the steps that teachers and other school staff members should take to ensure that they are appropriately and effectively supervising students' behaviors.

Choosing the Right System for Your Building

Some of the factors that should be taken into consideration when developing and adopting an anti-bullying policy for your school are:

1. **Age:** Disciplinary consequences and positive reinforcement should be age-appropriate. Loss of recess time may be an appropriate consequence for elementary students who bully but will likely be meaningless to middle and high school students.

2. **Fit:** The policy should fit into the existing values and structure of the community.

3. **Relevance:** The policy should be relevant and meaningful to the school community.

Negative Consequences for Problematic Behavior

Specific consequences should be established for bullying behaviors based on the severity and number of offenses. Examples of disciplinary rubrics can be found in chapter 6. Examples of consequences include verbal and/or written warnings, loss of privileges (such as recess time), informing the parent(s)/guardian(s) about the student's behavior, in-school suspension, mandatory attendance in anti-bullying awareness classes, a parent/guardian meeting with school officials, restitution, and, in cases of repeated and severe actions, suspension, expulsion, or a referral to law enforcement.

BRINGING POLICIES TO LIFE IN THE CLASSROOM

It's All about the People

Without commitment and action, a policy is nothing more than words on paper. Unfortunately, we can all think of examples of policies that have been drafted only to be relegated to the last pages of a student handbook or teacher training guide and never thought of again.

The purpose of an anti-bullying policy is to ensure that all students have a safe environment in which to learn. Hopefully, no one will argue against a student's right to be safe at school. If you, as a teacher or school staff member, believe it is your responsibility to help keep students safe at school, then you should be intrinsically motivated to breathe life into your anti-bullying policy. As you may recall from chapter 5, a positive and caring adult in a student's life can make a tremendous difference. You can be that adult!

Making Schoolwide Policies and Procedures Work in Your Classroom

Teachers should consistently and effectively implement the anti-bullying policies and procedures within the classroom setting. In addition to implementing the policies and procedures, the teachers should remember that the classroom setting is ideal for posting rules, holding classroom discussions, and practicing anti-bullying skills through role playing. Please refer to chapters 4 and 6 for more information about classroom rules, class discussions, and role playing.

SAMPLE ANTI-BULLYING POLICIES

Ohio's Department of Education and Bully Police provide two excellent examples of anti-bullying policies. You can find them online at ode.ohio .gov and bullypolice.org.

Best Practice Strategies for Bullying Prevention and Intervention

The U.S. Department of Health and Human Services' "Stop Bullying Now" campaign has identified 10 "best practice" strategies for bullying prevention and intervention (stopbullying.gov/community/tip_sheets/best_practices.pdf). These are effective principles that school officials can adopt to ensure that they are effectively and efficiently addressing the issue of bullying within their schools. The 10 best practice principles are:

1. Focus on the social environment of the school.
In order to reduce bullying, it is important to change the social climate of the school and the social norms with regards to bullying. This requires the efforts of everyone in the school environment—teachers, administrators, counselors, school nurses, school librarians, other nonteaching staff (such as bus drivers, custodians, and/or cafeteria workers), parents, and students.

2. Assess bullying at your school.
Adults are not always good at estimating the nature and prevalence of bullying at their school. As a result, it can be quite useful to administer an anonymous questionnaire to students about bullying. A number of bullying prevention programs listed in appendix B include these measures.

3. Obtain staff and parent buy-in and support for bullying prevention.
Bullying prevention should not be the sole responsibility of any single individual at a school. To be most effective, bullying prevention efforts require buy-in from the majority of the staff and parents. However, bullying prevention efforts should still begin even if immediate buy-in from all is not achievable. Usually, more and more supporters will join the effort once they see what it is accomplishing.

4. Form a group to coordinate the school's bullying prevention activities.
Bullying prevention efforts seem to work best if a representative group from the school coordinates them. This coordinating team might include:

- An administrator.
- A teacher and a student from each grade.
- A member of the nonteaching staff.
- A school counselor or other school-based mental health professional.
- A parent.

The team should meet regularly to review findings from the school's survey; plan specific bullying prevention activities; motivate staff, students, and parents; and ensure that the efforts continue over time.

5. Provide training for school staff and students in bullying prevention.
All administrators, faculty, staff, and students at a school should be trained in bullying prevention and intervention. In-service training can help staff members better understand the nature of bullying and its effects, how to respond if they observe bullying, and how to work with others at the school to help prevent bullying.

6. Establish and enforce school rules and policies related to bullying.

Developing simple, clear rules about bullying can help ensure that students are aware of adults' expectations that they not bully others and that they help students who are bullied. School rules and policies should be posted and discussed with students and parents. Appropriate positive and negative consequences should be developed.

7. Increase adult supervision in hot spots for bullying.

Bullying tends to thrive in locations where adults are not present or are not watchful. Adults should look for creative ways to increase adult presence in locations that students identify as hot spots.

8. Intervene consistently and appropriately when you see bullying.

Observed or suspected bullying should never be ignored by adults. All school staff should learn effective strategies to intervene on the spot to stop bullying. Certain staff members should be designated to hold sensitive, separate follow-up meetings with students who are bullied and with students who bully. Staff members should involve parents/guardians whenever possible.

9. Devote some class time to bullying prevention.

Students can benefit if teachers set aside a regular period of time (for example, 20 to 30 minutes each week or every other week) to discuss bullying and improving peer relations. These meetings can help teachers keep their fingers on the pulse of students' concerns, allow time for discussions about bullying and the harm that it can cause, and provide tools for students to address bullying problems. Anti-bullying messages can also be incorporated throughout the school curriculum.

10. Continue these efforts.

There should be no end date for bullying prevention activities. Bullying prevention should be continued over time and woven into the fabric of the school environment.

This handout may be reproduced for educational, noncommercial uses only (with this copyright line). From *The Right to Be Safe: Putting an End to Bullying Behavior* by Cricket Meehan, Ph.D. Copyright © 2011 Search Institute®, Minneapolis, MN; 877-240-7251 ext. 1; www.search-institute.org. All rights reserved. Adapted with permission from "Best Practices in Bullying Prevention and Intervention." Copyright © 2010 U.S. Department of Health and Human Services/ Health Resources and Services Administration, stopbullyingnow.hrsa.gov.

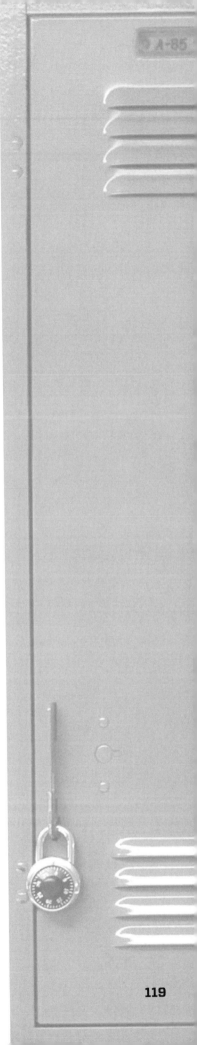

APPENDIX A

A History of the Definitions of Bullying

In order to systematically study the complex phenomenon of bullying, researchers need to define bullying behaviors in specific and precise terms. It is the agreement on and use of a consistent, precise definition that allows us to know that we are referring to the same thing when we discuss bullying. Empirical definitions describing bullying behavior have only begun to emerge in the last 40 years. During the 1970s, some of the earliest definitions were developed in Europe using the Scandinavian term *mobbning* (in English: *mobbing*). Peter-Paul Heinemann, a German-born Swedish medical physician, defined *mobbning* as "group violence against a deviant individual that occurs suddenly and subsides suddenly." Heinemann's definition referred to group behavior that occurs accidentally or circumstantially (for example, group violence that escalates due to anger or frustration against an individual).

Anatol Pikas, a Swedish psychologist, and Dan Olweus, a prominent bullying researcher at the University of Bergen in Norway, argued that circumstantial group violence motivated by intense negative emotions does not capture the essence of bullying behavior. In 1991, Olweus dropped his use of Heinemann's *mobbning* definition and adopted the term *bullying* instead, using it to refer not only to group violence but also to violence perpetrated by a single individual against others. According to Olweus's revised 1991 definition: "A person is being bullied or victimized when he or she is exposed, repeatedly and over time, to negative actions on the part of one or more other students."

Throughout the 1990s, researchers continued to refine their definitions of bullying. Many began to include other key factors to better describe the complex behaviors they were observing. These additional factors included different forms of bullying behavior (such as physical, verbal, indirect, and relational aggression), an intentionality on the part of the student(s) engaging in the behavior to do harm to others (that is, hurtful behavior that is done on purpose), an imbalance of power and control between the parties involved, and a myriad of consequences (physical, psychological, and social) associated with the behavior. A historical timeline of bullying definitions is included below.

MOST COMMONLY ACCEPTED AND USED DEFINITION OF BULLYING

Consolidating the previous decades of research into a single statement, in 1999 Olweus developed the following definition of bullying:

> *A person is bullied when he or she is exposed, repeatedly and over time, to negative actions on the part of one or more other persons, and he or she has difficulty defending himself or herself.*

Olweus's definition is arguably the most widely accepted and used definition of bullying throughout the world, and it captures precise and distinct components of bullying behavior.

A History of the Definition of Bullying

Heinemann (1973)

• Used the Scandinavian term *mobbning* (English: *mobbing*): "Mobbing is group violence against a deviant individual that occurs suddenly and subsides suddenly."

Olweus (1978)

• Used the original term *mobbning* and the group violence definition.

Pikas (1989)

• Defined bullying as both "(a) a single bully attacking an individual or group, or (b) a gang of bullies (sometimes with a leader, sometimes without a leader) attacking an individual or group."

• Argued that *mobbing* refers to the second (group violence) definition.

Olweus (1991)

• Adopted the word *bullying* instead of *mobbing* and used the following definition: "A person is being bullied or victimized when he or she is exposed, repeatedly and over time, to negative actions on the part of one or more other students."

Smith and Thompson (1991)

- Defined bullying as a subset of aggressive behavior that is intentional and intended to harm the other person/people physically or psychologically.
- Identified different forms of bullying, including direct physical aggression, indirect aggression, and direct verbal aggression.
- Identified three criteria that distinguish bullying: (1) it is unprovoked, (2) it occurs repeatedly, and (3) the bully is stronger or perceived to be stronger than the victim.

Dodge (1991)

- Defined bullying as a subset of aggression with two subtypes: (1) proactive aggression and (2) reactive aggression.
- Proactive aggression is directed at a victim to obtain a desired outcome, such as gaining property, power, or affiliation.
- Reactive aggression is directed at the victim as a result of an aversive (unpleasant) event that elicited anger or frustration on the part of the perpetrator.

Björkqvist, Lagerspetz, and Kaukiainen (1992)

- Defined bullying as a subset of aggression with four subtypes: (1) indirect aggression, (2) direct physical aggression, (3) direct verbal aggression, and (4) withdrawal.
- Indirect aggression, such as gossiping, suggesting shunning of another person, spreading vicious rumors as revenge, breaking contact with the person in question, and becoming friends with someone else as revenge.
- Direct physical aggression, such as tripping, taking things from another person, kicking and striking, taking revenge in games, and pushing and shoving.
- Direct verbal aggression, such as name-calling, profanity, trying to make the other person look stupid, and arguing.
- Withdrawal, such as sulking, withdrawing from the situation, and pretending not to know the person.

Whitney and Smith (1993)

- Defined bullying as "an aggressive act, with an imbalance of power that has some element of repetition, and can be physical, verbal, or indirect."

Farrington (1993)

- Defined bullying as "repeated oppression, physical or psychological, of a less powerful person by a more powerful person."

Smith and Sharp (1994)

- Defined bullying as the systematic abuse of power.
- "A student is being bullied or picked on when another student says nasty and unpleasant things to him or her. It is also bullying when a student is hit, kicked, threatened, locked inside a room, sent nasty notes, and when no one ever talks to him."

Rivers and Smith (1994)

- Identified three subtypes of bullying, including (1) direct physical, (2) direct verbal, and (3) indirect.
- Direct physical (physical hurt, for example, hitting and kicking or taking someone's belongings)
- Direct verbal (threatening or calling people names)
- Indirect (spreading rumors or socially excluding people)

Crick and Grotpeter (1995)

- Defined bullying as a subset of aggressive behaviors that are intended to hurt or harm others.
- "When attempting to inflict harm on peers (i.e., aggressing), children do so in ways that best thwart or damage the goals that are valued by their respective gender peer groups."

Crick and Grotpeter (1996)

- Coined the term *relational aggression.*
- Relational aggression is defined as aggression directed at damaging a relationship.

Galen and Underwood (1997)

- Defined bullying as a subset of aggression with two critical features:
  1. Aggressive behavior must be perceived negatively by the victim.
  2. Aggressive behavior must be intentional, where the aggressor is described as desirous of hurting or destroying the victim physically or psychologically.

Olweus (1999)

- Defined bullying as being characterized by three key components: (1) aggressive behavior or intentional harm-doing, (2) carried out repeatedly and over time, and (3) an imbalance of power within an interpersonal relationship.

- Identified three forms of negative actions: (1) direct verbal attacks (saying mean and unpleasant things or calling a student hurtful names), (2) physical attacks (hitting, kicking, shoving), and (3) indirect psychological methods (such as deliberately excluding a student from a social group).

Rigby (2002)

- Defined bullying with a formula: "Bullying = A desire to hurt a person or group + hurtful action + an imbalance of power + (typically) repetition + an unjust use of power + satisfaction for the aggressor + a sense of being hurt on the part of the target."

APPENDIX B

Evidence-Based Bullying Prevention Programs

In many cases, schools choose to implement evidence-based bullying prevention programs. These programs are typically comprehensive in nature, with a focus on changing the school's culture and climate regarding bullying and/or providing a set of lessons or a curriculum to raise students' awareness about bullying and teach them skills to reduce and/or prevent bullying.

All anti-bullying programs should be able to achieve the outcome of reducing bullying. Other outcomes that programs may achieve include:

- Decreases in behavioral problems.

- Decreases in violence.

- Increases in social competence.

- Increases in emotional competence.

- Increases in positive peer relationships.

- Increases in academic achievement.

An evidence-based program has been proved to achieve identified outcomes in a study in which the program was implemented with fidelity.

The following section describes programs that have been rigorously examined and proved to achieve intended outcomes with a broad group of students. Each of the programs listed here has received recognition from a nationally recognized organization that vets evidence-based programs.

Al's Pals: Kids Making Healthy Choices is a school-based prevention program that seeks to develop social and emotional skills such as self-control, problem solving, and healthy decision making in children ages 3 through 8 in preschool, kindergarten, and grade 1. The program has demonstrated success in (1) increasing students' social competence, (2) increasing students' prosocial behaviors, (3) decreasing students' antisocial behaviors, and (4) decreasing students' aggressive behaviors.

Brief Strategic Family Therapy (BSFT) is designed to (1) prevent, reduce, and/or treat adolescent behavior problems such as drug use, conduct problems, delinquency, sexually risky behavior, aggressive/violent behavior, and association with antisocial peers; (2) improve prosocial behaviors such as school attendance and performance; and (3) improve family functioning, including effective parental leadership and management, positive parenting, and parental involvement with the child, his peers, and school.

Building Assets—Reducing Risks (BARR) is a multifaceted school-based prevention program from Search Institute designed to decrease the incidence of substance abuse (tobacco, alcohol, and other drugs), academic failure, truancy, and disciplinary incidents among grade 9 youth. The program has demonstrated success in (1) reducing class failure, (2) reducing bullying at school, and (3) increasing students' connectedness to school.

The Olweus Bullying Prevention Program, developed by Dr. Dan Olweus, a research professor of psychology at the University of Bergen in Norway, is arguably one of the most well-known and well-respected school-based bullying prevention programs in existence. Prompted by a national campaign against bullying by the Norwegian Ministry of Education, Dr. Olweus developed the program in response to the tragic suicides of three Norwegian schoolchildren who had been severely bullied by their peers. Dr. Olweus has conducted multiple program evaluation studies and has refined and expanded the program. It is now widely used in many countries, including the United States and Canada.

The Olweus Bullying Prevention Program has four main areas in which the program takes place: at a schoolwide level, within classrooms, at an individual student level, and within the community at large. Some of the outcomes that schools can expect include:

- Fifty percent or more reductions in student reports of being bullied and bullying others.

- Reductions in student reports of school bullying, vandalism, school violence, fighting, theft, and truancy.

 F.A.Q.

Many teachers often ask, "Why is it so important for a program to be evidence-based?" Although there are likely many bullying prevention programs out there that are not officially recognized as evidence-based but that do make a difference, most anti-bullying experts would recommend that you choose an evidence-based program if that is an option. *Evidence-based* means that the program has been rigorously tested with large samples through research-controlled studies and was found to be effective in achieving identified outcomes.

F.A.Q.

Some teachers want to know: "Why are some programs not designated as evidence-based?" One reason could be that the program has been tested but shown to be ineffective in achieving desired outcomes. If this is the case, this program should be avoided. A second reason could be that the program has never been evaluated to determine if it is achieving its intended outcomes. Programs like this should be selected and implemented with caution. If you choose a program like this, it would be very valuable to implement an evaluation plan to determine if the program is working for your school. A third reason could be that the program has been evaluated in individual settings (like a school or classroom) but not on a larger scale. If the program was initially successful, it is likely considered a promising program. If you select a program like this, be aware that you may or may not achieve the same results as with evidence-based programs.

- Improvements in classroom social climate, including improved order and discipline, more positive social relationships, and more positive attitudes toward schoolwork and school.

- Greater support for students who are bullied.

- More effective interventions for students who bully.

Currently the program has been evaluated for use with elementary and middle school students, but steps are being taken to modify the program for use with high school students. For more information about the Olweus Bullying Prevention Program, visit olweus.org.

Second Step: A Violence Prevention Curriculum is a school-based violence prevention curriculum for students in pre-K through grade 8. The Second Step curriculum teaches students social and emotional skills, which support academic learning. The program's lessons align with academic content standards, character education principles, and Head Start performance standards. Second Step has been proved to increase students' social competence, prosocial skills, and positive behaviors. It has been proved to reduce aggression, anxiety, and depression among students. More information about the Second Step program can be found at cfchildren.org/programs/ssp/overview.

APPENDIX C

U.S. Federal and State Laws Regarding Bullying: Implications for Schools

Teachers and school staff should be aware of the laws within their states and local areas to ensure that they act within the confines of the law regarding bullying and cyberbullying. Teachers should be aware of their mandated reporter status and how that plays out in cases of bullying. Whenever possible, professional development training that discusses these important topics should be sought out. Understanding your legal responsibilities will help reduce your liability in situations of student abuse.

FEDERAL LEGISLATION

Since January 8, 2002, the Safe and Drug-Free Schools and Communities Act (SDFSCA) has been in place to keep our children safe. SDFSCA has four overarching goals: (1) to prevent violence in schools, (2) to prevent illegal use of substances (that is, alcohol, tobacco, and illicit drugs), (3) to involve parents and community members, and (4) to create safe and drug-free learning environments that will help students achieve academically. The Office of Safe and Drug-Free Schools works to create a drug-free school environment and to prevent violent, aggressive behaviors such as bullying at school.

The Office of Safe and Drug-Free Schools provides financial assistance for drug and violence prevention efforts, helps formulate

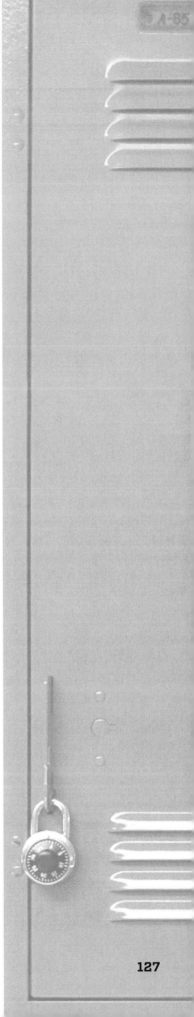

program policies related to violence and drug prevention, and coordinates with other federal agencies on violence and drug prevention issues. For more information about the Office of Safe and Drug-Free Schools, visit www2.ed.gov/about/offices/list/osdfs/index.html.

STATE LAWS AGAINST BULLYING

In addition to the federal SDFSCA, most states have adopted anti-bullying legislation. In the United States (as of May 2011), 46 states have anti-bullying legislation in place, according to Bully Police, a watchdog organization that advocates for children who are bullied (bullypolice.org). The only states that do not have anti-bullying legislation in place are Hawaii, Michigan, Montana, and South Dakota (shown as shaded).

Timeline of Passage of Anti-Bullying Legislation by State

- 1999: GA
- 2000: NH
- 2001: CO, LA, MS, OR, WV
- 2002: CT, NJ, OK, WA
- 2003: AR, CA, RI
- 2004: VT
- 2005: AZ, IN, MD, VA, TX, TN, ME, NV
- 2006: ID, SC, AK, NM
- 2007: DE, IA, IL, KS, MN, OH, PA
- 2008: NE, KY, UT, FL
- 2009: NC, WY, AL
- 2010: MA, WI, NY, MO
- 2011: ND

BULLY POLICE GRADING FOR STATE LEGISLATION

Bully Police is a watchdog organization that advocates for children who are bullied and reports on state anti-bullying laws. In fact, Bully Police reviews each anti-bullying law from every state that has passed (or has pending) anti-bullying legislation. The organization assigns a letter grade (A, B, C, D, or F) to the state's legislation based on 12 criteria.

A number of states' anti-bullying laws have received excellent grades from Bully Police. Delaware, Florida, Georgia, Kentucky, Massachusetts, Maryland, New Hampshire, North Dakota, Virginia, and Wyoming have all received A++ ratings for their excellent laws, which emphasize providing counseling for students who have been bullied *and* have a cyberbullying clause. States that do not have anti-bullying laws—Hawaii, Michigan, Montana, and South Dakota—received a grade of F. Some states, like Michigan, have pending legislation that, when passed, will receive high marks.

For more information about grades that individual states have received, visit bullypolice.org and click on a state. In addition to grades, an overview and a complete listing of the laws are included for review.

BULLYING LEGAL CASES

In recent years, there have been an increasing number of litigious cases brought before judges across the United States with regard to bullying and cyberbullying situations. Unfortunately, the results of these cases have been mixed. This inconsistency has led to frustration on the part of many school officials about their legal responsibility in protecting students from bullying and cyberbullying.

In March 2010, a Michigan court ordered the Hudson Area School District to pay $800,000 in damages to a student who was bullied, citing deliberate indifference on the part of the teachers and staff, but the jury's decision was later overturned on appeal. In two similar cases, juries ordered school districts to pay compensation to students who had been sexually harassed. In 2000, Spencer County Public School District in Kentucky was ordered to pay a student $220,000 following student-on-student sexual harassment. In 2005, Tonganoxie Unified School District in Kansas was ordered to pay a student $250,000 for being deliberately indifferent during the student's five-year history of being bullied and sexually harassed at school. The juries in both of these cases felt that the schools were irresponsible and indifferent and should have done more to protect the students.

The inconsistency that currently exists in legal decisions makes it very difficult for school officials to know how to handle bullying situations. Another area that is controversial is the search and seizure of electronic devices by school officials. Many legal experts now warn school officials that they can be charged with possessing child pornography if they seize a student's phone and find evidence of "sexting" on the device while searching it. Under many state laws, possession of semi-nude or nude photos of a minor is considered a sexual offense (and in some cases, a felony). School officials in these states are being advised to involve law enforcement officials when the need for search and seizure of electronic devices arises.

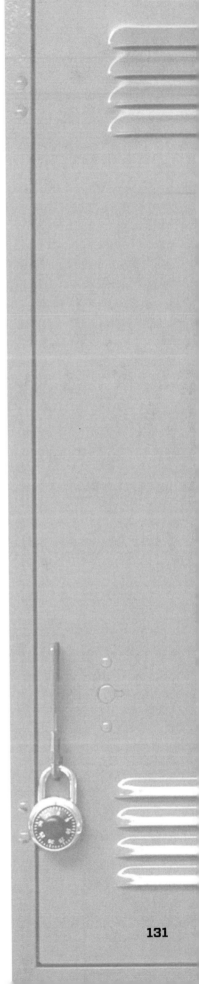

APPENDIX D

Finding Funding for Your Bullying Prevention Efforts

When selecting resources to use in your anti-bullying efforts, it is important to make sure that those resources support the values and beliefs of your school and community regarding violence prevention. For example, understanding that bullying is a behavior is a very important distinction to make, as we have addressed in previous sections of this book. Many resources that exist tend to pathologize students as bullies and victims. Hopefully, the discussions in this book have helped you understand why such language can be dangerous and unhelpful. That being said, resources that you select to use with your students should focus on bullying as a behavior—a behavior that can be changed.

Take time to review the materials that you are presented with to determine if they complement your beliefs and views about bullying behaviors. Decide if they are culturally appropriate for the group that you intend to use them with. Ensure that the lessons and messages are meaningful and relevant to your students. By taking the time to select appropriate materials, you will help ensure that those materials will be used successfully in your efforts to reduce and/or prevent bullying at your school and in your community.

GETTING BUY-IN FROM THE COMMUNITY

When bringing anti-bullying efforts into a school system, there is often resistance from many different groups of people. Sometimes the resistance comes in the form of not wanting something else to add to an already overflowing list of responsibilities. Other times, the resistance arises because individuals do not believe that there is a bullying problem in the first place. And yet another reason why resistance may exist is because individuals are unsure what to do to address the problem (that is, they lack skills or resources).

The first step in getting buy-in from everyone who will be affected is concretely identifying the existence of the problem. It is important to use whatever evidence you have to show people that bullying is a concern at the school. National statistics demonstrating how many students are directly involved in bullying can help, but if you are able to show the specific percentages from your school, you will have a much more persuasive argument. Information can come from disciplinary or behavioral referrals, self-report survey data, or anecdotal stories of specific incidents of bullying.

The next step is to identify concrete, tangible solutions to the problem that can be implemented at your school. Many different types of solutions have been addressed throughout this book, including disciplinary procedures for students who bully, positive peer relationship-building techniques, and supportive adult role models who can support a positive school culture and climate. Remember that bullying is a repeated and often long-term problem that will likely require clear, consistent, effective, and sustained efforts to stop it and prevent it from occurring.

Once those solutions have been identified, everyone should be provided with ample opportunities to practice and master the skills needed to implement the solutions. When people feel confident about what they can do to make a difference, they are much more likely to actually take steps to make that difference a reality. Choose solutions that can be easily implemented within the school setting. Staff should be encouraged to use techniques that do not require vast amounts of their time and take away from their already existing responsibilities. One advantage of addressing bullying and other violent behaviors within the school setting is that schools with a positive school culture and climate do not have to waste valuable teaching time addressing students' disruptive, problematic behaviors.

U.S. FEDERAL FUNDING

The Office of Safe and Drug-Free Schools was established to create safe schools, respond to crises, prevent drug abuse and violence, ensure the health and well-being of students, and promote the development of good character and citizenship. It administers the following grant programs to assist schools in this mission:

1. Health, Mental Health, Environmental Health, and Physical Education

2. Drug-Violence Prevention—State Programs

3. Drug-Violence Prevention—National Programs

4. Character and Civic Education

5. Policy and Cross-Cutting Programs

6. Safe and Drug-Free Schools and Communities Advisory Committee

Information about each program is available at www2.ed.gov/about/offices/list/osdfs/index.html.

In addition to the Office of Safe and Drug-Free Schools, other federal entities periodically provide funding for schools:

- The Administration for Children and Families (ACF)

- Catalog of Federal Domestic Assistance (CFDA)

- Centers for Disease Control and Prevention (CDC)

- Healthy Youth Funding Database (HY-FUND)

- Department of Education Forecast of Funding

- Department of Education Grants

- No Child Left Behind—Title I

- National Institute of Mental Health (NIMH)

- Office of Juvenile Justice and Delinquency Prevention (OJJDP)

- Character Education Partnership

- Public Education Network

- Safe and Drug-Free Schools and Communities (SDFSC)

- Safe Schools, Healthy Students (SS/HS)

- Substance Abuse and Mental Health Services Administration (SAMHSA)

- Suicide Prevention Resource Center (SPRC)

- U.S. Department of Health and Human Services (HHS)

Many of the funding opportunities for these entities are available at grants.gov.

STATE FUNDING

Many state-level departments typically have a vested interest in ensuring that their students have a safe and secure place in which to learn. State departments of education, mental health, health, and juvenile justice/delinquency prevention are all entities that may have the ability to work with school districts to reduce and prevent violence and abuse within school settings. In some cases, these entities may also have funding available for dissemination to schools within their jurisdiction. School officials can contact your state's departments to inquire about the possibility for support and/or funding assistance for your anti-bullying efforts.

FOUNDATIONS AND CENTERS

Clearinghouse websites exist that identify community foundations that support schools' anti-bullying and violence prevention efforts. Both the Council on Foundations and the Foundation Directory Online can be used to search for funding opportunities in your state:

- The Council on Foundations's clearinghouse list can be found at cof.org. Click on "Community Foundations," then look under the "Resources" section to find the "Community Foundation Locator."

- The Foundation Directory Online's clearinghouse list can be found at foundationcenter.org. Click on "Find Funders." Under "Identify Funding Sources," you will find the "Foundation Directory Online." A subscription is needed to access this resource.

Many foundations offer funding to schools to support violence prevention efforts and activities. Typically, these foundations offer funding to organizations that are within the service and/or catchment area. If any of the below-mentioned foundations are in your area, it may be worthwhile to investigate whether or not they have current grant funding opportunities available to support your anti-bullying efforts. The foundations that have a history of funding violence prevention efforts and activities are:

- The Allstate Foundation: allstate.com/foundation.aspx

- The Annenberg Foundation: annenbergfoundation.org

- The Braitmayer Foundation: braitmayerfoundation.org

- Charles Lafitte Foundation: charleslafitte.org

- Fundsnet Services Online: fundsnetservices.com

- Garth Brooks Teammates for Kids Foundation: teammatesforkids.com

- Hasbro Community Relations: hasbro.com/corporate/community-relations

- The Lawrence Foundation: thelawrencefoundation.org

- The Macy's Foundation: macysinc.com/community

- Newman's Own® Foundation: newmansownfoundation.org

- Office Depot Community Relations: community.officedepot.com/odchia.asp

- Public Education Network: publiceducation.org

- Sprint Character Education Grant Program: sprint.com/responsibility/education/character

- Wells Fargo Corporate Giving: wellsfargo.com/wachovia/foundation

CIVIC AND FRATERNAL ORGANIZATIONS

These civic and fraternal organizations fund anti-bullying and violence prevention opportunities:

- American Legion Auxiliary: legion-aux.org

- The Association of Junior Leagues International, Inc.: ajli.org

- Kiwanis International: sites.kiwanis.org/kiwanis/en/home.aspx

- Lions Clubs International: lionsclubs.org/EN/index.php

- The Rotary Foundation: rotary.org/en/Pages/ridefault.aspx

- United States Junior Chamber Jaycees: usjaycees.org

- United Way of America: liveunited.org

LOCAL BUSINESSES

In many cases, local businesses are looking for philanthropic opportunities within the local community. Those businesses could include retail businesses, restaurants, family-owned businesses, places of worship, and health/mental health organizations, among others. When schools have a social, emotional, and behavioral health project that needs support and funding, school officials can develop a request for support letter that they can use to approach local businesses. A request for support should include the identified need within the school (that is, the need to reduce bullying), the way the proposed project will address that need, the specific resources that will be needed to implement the project (funding, volunteers, materials), and the specific resources/funding that are requested from the local business. If possible, it is nice to identify ways in which the local business can participate in the anti-bullying efforts—for example, by providing the business with the school's anti-bullying rules so it can post them in its place of business, or having a staff member from the business come to the school to talk with students about an anti-bullying message.

TIPS FOR SUCCESSFUL GRANT WRITING

The Associated Grant Makers' website, which can be found at agm connect.org, has a wonderful section on grant seeking, grant writing, and fund-raising resources. Click on "For Grant Seekers" and go to the "Key Resources" section. In the "Grant Seeking, Grant Writing" section, there are many valuable resources that can assist you as you look for and then write applications for grant opportunities.

CLASSROOM FUND-RAISING IDEAS

Fundsnet Services Online's clearinghouse list can be found at funds netservices.com. Click on "Fundraising Resources" for an extensive list of fund-raising opportunities.

RESOURCES

Here you will find resources that can be used in classroom and school settings to combat bullying. Books, workbooks, websites and online resources, public service announcements, anti-bullying campaigns, videos, electronic resources, and tool kits are listed.

BOOKS AND WORKBOOKS

The following books and workbooks cover a variety of topics that are important to help students build positive character traits. Positive character traits are protective factors against bullying and other aggressive behaviors. The traits identified below are self-control, friendliness, safety, compassion, courteousness, being positive, readiness and responsibility, good citizenship, and teamwork. Books that are appropriate for elementary, middle, and high school students have been identified for each of the character traits. This list was compiled by Miami University undergraduate students Emily Cameron, Hilary Denune, Danielle Kohler, Marianne Maczko, and Jessica Overdorf.

Self-Control

Elementary School:

- *In Control: A Book of Games to Teach Self-Control Skills* by Lawrence E. Shapiro
- *It's Hard to Be Five: Learning How to Work My Control Panel* by Jamie Lee Curtis
- *Sunny the Greedy Goat Learns the Value of Self-Control* by Ethel Barrett

Middle/High School:

- *Anna's Choice* by Catherine Carter and Gail Pittman
- *I'm Not Bad, I'm Just Mad* by Lawrence E. Sharpiro, Zach Pelta-Heller, and Anna F. Greenwald
- *Out of Control* by Norma Fox Mazer

Friendliness

Elementary School:

- *The Friendly Four* by Eloise Greenfield and Jan Spivey Gilchrist
- *Have You Filled a Bucket Today?* by Carol McCloud
- *What Are Friends For?* by Marsha Karzmer

Middle/High School:

- *Friendly Foes: A Look at Political Parties* (How Government Works) by Elaine Landau
- *Growing Up with a Bucket Full of Happiness: Three Rules for a Happier Life* by Carol McCloud

Safety

Elementary School:

- *Be Careful and Stay Safe* (Learning to Get Along) by Cheri J. Meiners
- *The Kids' Guide to Working Out Conflicts: How to Keep Cool, Stay Safe, and Get Along* by Naomi Drew
- *Watch Out for Banana Peels and Other Important Sesame Street Safety Tips* by Sarah Albee

Middle/High School:

- *Beyond Safe Boundaries* by Margaret Sacks
- *The Safe Zone: A Kid's Guide to Personal Safety* by Donna Chaiet, Francine Russell, and Lillian Gee
- *Stay Safe! How You Can Keep Out of Harm's Way* (Health Zone) by Sara Nelson and Jack Desrocher

Compassion

Elementary School:

- *Gregory Is Grouchy: And Other Really Good Reasons to Be Compassionate* (Kirkland Street Kids) by Sandy Silverthorne
- *Lily and the Paper Man* by Rebecca Upjohn

- *Teaching Children Empathy, the Social Emotion: Lessons, Activities and Reproducible Worksheets (K–6) That Teach How to Step into Others' Shoes* by Tonia Caselman

Middle/High School:

- *A Cup of Cold Water: The Compassion of Nurse Edith Cavell* by Christine Farenhorst
- *The Robber Chief: A Tale of Vengeance and Compassion* by W. W. Rowe
- *A Trilogy . . . featuring Big Oak Mega Buck! Ella's Compassion & the Knock at Our Door* by Phil Kunz

Courteousness

Elementary School:

- *Be Nice, Nanette!* by Sarah Willson and Elizabeth Brandt
- *Let's Talk About Being Helpful Book and CD* by Joy Berry
- *The Nice Book* by David Ezra Stein

Middle/High School:

- *The Courteous Cad* by Catherine Palmer
- *Helpful Henry* by Ruth Brown
- *Let's Talk about Being Helpful* by Jim Arnosky

Being Positive

Elementary School:

- *I Believe in Me: A Book of Affirmations* by Connie Bowen
- *Phil the Pill and Friends: Making Positive Choices* by M. Ann Machen Pritchard
- *Proud to Be You: The Positive Identity Assets* (Adding Assets) by Pamela Espeland and Elizabeth Verdick

Middle/High School:

- *Drama Queens (& Kings): Positive Ways for Tweens to Act Out* by Marcia Joslin Stoner
- *Knowing and Doing What's Right: The Positive Values Assets* (Adding Assets) by Pamela Espeland and Elizabeth Verdick
- *Live It: Optimism* by Robert Walker

Readiness and Responsibility

Elementary School:

- *Don't Behave Like You Live in a Cave* by Elizabeth Verdick
- *I Can Be Responsible* (Doing the Right Thing) by Jenette Donovan Guntly and Priscilla Burris
- *The Little Book of Values: Educating Children to Become Thinking, Responsible and Caring Citizens* (Independent Thinking Series) by Julie Duckworth and Ian Gilbert

Middle/High School:

- *Accept and Value Each Person* by Cheri J. Meiners
- *Being Responsible* by Mike Gillespie, Steven McCullough, and Mike Nappa
- *Character-Building Activities: Teaching Responsibility, Interaction and Group Dynamics* by Judy Demers

Good Citzenship

Elementary School:

- *Good Citizenship Counts* by Marie Bender
- *We Live Here Too! Kids Talk About Good Citizenship* by Nancy Loewen and Wesley Omarr
- *Working Together: Learning about Cooperation and Citizenship* by Regina Burch

Middle/High School:

- *Citizenship* by Ann-Marie Kishel
- *The Good Citizen* by David B. Batstone and Eduardo Mendieta
- *The Good Citizen: How a Younger Generation Is Reshaping American Politics* by Russell J. Dalton

Teamwork

Elementary School:

- *Let's Play as a Team!* by P. K. Hallinan
- *Teamwork Saves the Day* by Josh Seliq
- *What a Team! Together Everyone Achieves More* by Fran Shaw and Ryuichi Sakamoto

Middle/High School:

- *Team Challenges: 170+ Group Activities to Build Cooperation, Communication, and Creativity* by Kris Bordessa

- *Teamwork at Camp Tioga* by Marsha Hubler
- *Winning with Teamwork: Quotations to Inspire the Power of Teamwork* by Katherine Karvelas

VIDEOS

Videos can be a powerful tool to use in the classroom with students. They provide the students with powerful imagery and messages that can serve as catalysts for additional classroom discussion.

- *Let's Fight It Together: Cyberbullying Film* available at: digizen.org/ resources/cyberbullying/films/uk/lfit-film.aspx. This is a nine-minute video that has a "Responding to Cyberbullying" lesson plan that teachers can use after playing the video. This is from the digizen.org website (see below).

- CommonSenseMedia has a new digital citizenship curriculum with videos for middle school students available at commonsensemedia .org. Click on "Educators" to find the "Digital Literacy and Citizen-ship Curriculum." (Register as an educator to have access to the materials.) The "Privacy & Digital Footprints" unit has three videos for students: (1) *Digital Footprint,* (2) *Eva's Story,* and (3) *Brittney's Story.*

- The Ad Council has a video called *Cyberbullying—Talent Show* available at YouTube: youtube.com/watch?v=3gN84KW7RuU.

WEBSITES

Many websites provide extensive information for teachers, students, and parents/guardians about bullying and cyberbullying. Below are some of the most useful and comprehensive websites that address the topic of bullying. All of them provide resources and tools that teachers, students, and parents can use in their quest to better understand bul-lying and ultimately address problematic bullying behaviors.

Stopbullyingnow.hrsa.gov

The U.S. Department of Health and Human Services' Health Resources and Services Administration (HRSA) developed the "Stop Bullying Now!" campaign to help kids and adults know what they can do to stop bullying. The website (stopbullyingnow.hrsa.gov) is broken into two major sections: "What Kids Can Do" and "What Adults Can Do."

The "What Kids Can Do" section includes a definition of bullying, an explanation about why kids bully, warning signs, and the effects of bullying. There are suggestions for what to do if you are being bullied, witnessing bullying, or bullying others. The website encourages young people to become leaders in their schools and communities by taking a stand against bullying behavior. The website has 12 animated webisodes that show a bullying scenario along with downloadable discussion questions for teachers to use in their classrooms. Each of the cast members has his or her own biography page in the "Meet the Cast" section. In addition, the website includes games that youth can play to help raise their awareness about bullying and learn skills for stopping it.

The "What Adults Can Do" section includes featured articles on topics such as cyberbullying and state laws on bullying. Information about children who bully, children who are bullied, what we know about bullying, and why adults should care is also available. Prevention and intervention techniques are discussed, and webcasts are available to download. Tips for selecting bullying-related programs and materials are included, as are sections on state laws regarding bullying and research studies and reports. Downloadable tip sheets on a variety of useful topics are available. There are sections for parents/family members, educators, health and safety professionals, law enforcement officers, mental health professionals, and youth advisors.

Stopbullyingnow.com

Stan Davis, who has worked as a social worker, a child/family therapist, and a school counselor, developed the Stopbullyingnow.com website to help stop bullying in schools and community settings. The site includes sections on identifying bullying; what does and does not work in bullying prevention/intervention; helping, supporting, and empowering involved youth; identifying bullying by teachers and school staff; best practices in bullying prevention; a summary for parents; resources, articles, research, books, videos, and CDs; trainings; and information about consulting with Mr. Davis.

Bullying.org

Bullying.org was created by Bill Beasley, a father and teacher who felt the need to take action following a school shooting at W. R. Myers High School in Alberta. He dedicated the site to Jason Lang, the student killed in the shooting. The website's purpose "is to eliminate bullying in our society by supporting individuals and organizations to take positive actions against bullying through the sharing of resources, and to guide and champion them in creating non-violent solutions to the challenges and problems associated with bullying." There is information about what bullying is, why people bully, why people are targeted, and what to do if you are bullied, witness bullying, or are bullying others. The website includes educational programs and resources for individuals, families, educational institutions, and organizations. The founder lists a series of presentations that he can provide (in person) to interested schools and organizations.

Pacer.org/bullying/index.asp

The Pacer Center's National Bullying Prevention Center website is available at pacer.org/bullying/index.asp. It encourages people to become engaged in anti-bullying efforts by joining an anti-bullying cause. There are educational materials on the website, including classroom instructional materials and activities. The site includes an "Introductory Toolkit for Raising Bullying Prevention and Awareness," along with a "Comprehensive Educational Toolkit" for both elementary and middle/high school classrooms.

Pacerteensagainstbullying.org

The Pacer Center has a website dedicated to teens against bullying. The Teens Against Bullying website interface is much more teen-friendly, with an iPod-like menu system and real teenagers discussing the topics.

Pacerkidsagainstbullying.org

The Pacer Center's Kids Against Bullying website has games, activities, contests, videos, stories, and information about what bullying is and how to stop it.

Digizen.org

The Digizen.org website provides information for educators, parents, and students about digital citizenship and how to be a responsible user of technology. The site includes a downloadable lesson plan on digital values and guidance on cyberbullying. There are several videos on a variety of cyberbullying topics.

ELECTRONIC RESOURCES

Curricula and e-books exist that address the topics of bullying and cyberbullying. Below are two free resources that are available.

- *Own Your Space—Keep Yourself and Your Stuff Safe Online* Digital Book for Teens by Linda McCarthy. This is a free, downloadable e-book written for teens to help them "own their own space" online. Parents and educators will also find this book useful to read. It is available at microsoft.com.

- The *Prevention-Intervention Services: Middle School Cyberbullying Curriculum* is available at seattleschools.org/area/prevention/cbms.xml.

TOOL KITS

Eyes on Bullying Toolkit

The Eyes on Bullying Toolkit, developed and written by Kim Storey, Ron Slaby, Melanie Adler, Jennifer Minotti, and Rachel Katz at Education Development Center, Inc., was designed to help adults understand the extent, seriousness, and dynamics of bullying; recognize and respond early and effectively to behaviors that can lead to bullying; learn about new, effective strategies for controlling bullying; prepare children to recognize and respond effectively to early bullying behavior; teach children how everyone—bullies, victims, bystanders, and supportive adults—can help control bullying; create an environment where everyone understands that bullying behaviors are unacceptable, harmful, and preventable; and empower yourself and children to actively intervene to prevent and stop bullying. It is a 43-page tool kit that can be downloaded free of charge at eyesonbullying.org/pdfs/toolkit.pdf.

Other Bullying Prevention Tool Kits

- Georgia Department of Education: doe.k12.ga.us/sia_titleiv .aspx?PageReq=SIABully
- Pacer Center: pacer.org/bullying/bpaw/toolkit.asp
- University of Western Sydney: uws.edu.au/equity_diversity/ equity_and_diversity/tools_and_resources/stop_bullying_toolkit
- Anti-Defamation League: adl.org/civil_rights/Anti-Bullying% 20Law%20Toolkit_2009.pdf
- Health Teacher: healthteacher.com/news/Article/1196

PUBLIC SERVICE ANNOUNCEMENTS

Public service announcements (PSAs) are a great way to introduce students to various bullying-related topics. Teachers can show PSAs in the classroom and then hold whole-class discussions about the messages that were addressed in the video. Some teachers have used national PSAs as examples for their students, asking them to develop and film their own PSAs. Some schools and districts have broadcast the student-created PSAs during National Bullying Awareness Month in October. The following are examples of widely available anti-bullying PSAs.

- Stop Homophobic Bullying: youtube.com/watch?v=xWiollKJWdo
- The Price of Silence: youtube.com/watch?v=wY7Gvq0P4hc
- QuantamShift.tv Bullying: quantumshift.tv/v/1200068714/

- Hellcats' PSA: entertainment.gather.com/viewArticle.action?articleId=281474978578742
- Anti-Bullying PSA: youtube.com/watch?v=DlSwfcxoNl0
- SchoolTube.com: schooltube.com/video/41b21c03182340c5b6f5/Bullying-PSA

ANTI-BULLYING CAMPAIGNS

On the national level, several anti-bullying campaigns have been launched. The following list identifies some of these campaigns. Throughout the United States, there are numerous local anti-bullying campaigns that have mirrored the efforts of the national campaigns.

- U.S. Health Resources and Services Administration's Stop Bullying Now! Campaign: stopbullyingnow.hrsa.gov
- NLDline Anti-Bullying Campaign: nldline.com/antibull.htm
- Pacer Center's Kids Against Bullying Campaign: pacerkidsagainstbullying.org/
- Pacer Center's Teens Against Bullying Campaign: pacerteensagainstbullying.org/
- "It Gets Better" Campaign: youtube.com/itgetsbetterproject

BIBLIOGRAPHY

Alberto, P. A., & Troutman, A. C. (1995). *Applied behavior analysis for teachers* (4th ed.). Englewood Cliffs, NJ: Merrill Publishing.

Aluede, O. (2006). Bullying in schools: A form of child abuse in schools. *Educational Research Quarterly, 30*(1), 37–49.

American Psychological Association (APA) (2010). Improving students' relationships with teachers to provide essential supports for learning: Teacher's modules. Retrieved September 27, 2010, from apa.org/education/k12/relationships.aspx.

Andreou, E. (2004). Bully/victim problems and their association with Machiavellianism and self-efficacy in Greek primary school children. *British Journal of Educational Psychology, 74*, 297–309.

Baker, J.A. (1998). Are we missing the forest for the trees? Considering the social context of school violence. *Journal of School Psychology, 36*, 29–44.

Baker, J.A., Terry, T., Bridger, R., & Winsor, A. (1997). Schools as caring communities: A relational approach to school reform. *School Psychology, 26*, 276–288.

Baker, M. (June 20, 2010). Parents try to help after Perkins boy's suicide; family says bullying was a factor. NewsOK (Oklahoma City, OK). Retrieved July 13, 2010, from newsok.com/article/3473418?searched=ty%20fields&custom_click=search.

Ballard, M., Tucky, A., & Remley, T.P. Jr. (1999). Bullying and violence: A proposed prevention program. *National Association of Secondary School Principals (NASSP) Bulletin*, 38–47.

Battistich, V., Schaps, E., & Wilson, N. (2004). Effects of an elementary school intervention on students' "connectedness" to school and social adjustment during middle school. *Journal of Primary Prevention, 24*(3), 243–262.

Beale, A.V. (2001). Bully busters: Using drama to empower students to take a stand against bullying behavior. *Professional School Counseling, 4,* 300–306.

Becker, W. C. (1986). *Applied psychology for teachers*. Chicago: Science Research Associates.

Berry, D., & O'Connor, E. (2009). Behavioral risk, teacher–child relationships, and social skill development across middle childhood: A child-by-environment analysis of change. *Journal of Applied Developmental Psychology, 31*(1), 1–14.

Birch, S. H., & Ladd, G. W. (1997). The teacher-child relationship and early school adjustment. *Journal of School Psychology, 55*(1), 61–79.

Björkqvist, K., Lagerspetz, K.M.J., & Kaukiainen, A. (1992). Do girls manipulate and boys fight? *Aggressive Behavior, 18,* 117–127.

Bond, L., Carlin, J.B., Thomas, L., Rubin, K., & Patton, G. (2001). Does bullying cause emotional problems? A prospective study of young teenagers. *British Medical Journal, 323,* 480–484.

Bosworth, K., Espelage, D.L., & Simon, T. (1999). Factors associated with bullying behavior in middle school students. *Journal of Early Adolescence, 19,* 341–362.

Bradshaw, C.P., Sawyer, A.L., & O'Brennan, L.M. (2007). Bullying and peer victimization at school: Perceptual differences between students and school staff. *School Psychology Review, 36*(3), 361–382.

Brockenbrough, K.K., Cornell, D.G., & Loper, A.B. (2002). Aggressive attitudes among victims of violence at school. *Education and Treatment of Children, 25,* 273–287.

Bullying (2010). In *Merriam-Webster Online Dictionary*. Retrieved June 12, 2010, from merriam-webster.com/dictionary/bullying.

Carney, A.G., & Merrell, K.W. (2001). Bullying in schools: Perspectives on understanding and preventing an international problem. *School Psychology International, 22,* 364–381.

Clarke, E. A., & Kiselica, M. S. (1997). A systematic counseling approach to the problem of bullying. *Elementary School Guidance and Counseling, 31,* 310–325.

Connell, J.P., & Wellborn, J.G. (1991). Competence, autonomy, and relatedness: A motivational analysis of self-system processes. In M.R. Gunnar & L.A. Sroufe (Eds.), *Self-processes in development: Minnesota Symposium on Child Psychology* (Vol. 23, 43–77). Hillside, NJ: Erlbaum.

Conolly, J.C., Hindmand, R., Jacobs, Y., & Gagnon, W.A. (1997). How schools promote violence. *Family Futures, 1*(1), 8–11.

Cornelius-White, J. (2007). Learner-centered teacher-student relationships are effective: A meta-analysis. *Review of Educational Research, 77*(1), 113–143.

Crick, N.R., & Grotpeter, J.K. (1995). Relational aggression, gender, and social-psychological adjustment. *Child Development, 66,* 710–722.

Crick, N.R., & Grotpeter, J.K. (1996). Children's treatment by peers: Victims of relational and overt aggression. *Development and Psychopathology, 8,* 367–380.

Deci, E.L., Vallerand, R.J., Pelletier, L.G., & Ryan, R.M. (1991). Motivation and education: The self-determination perspective. *Educational Psychologist, 26,* 324–346.

Dodge, K. A. (1991). The structure and function of reactive and proactive aggression. In D. J. Pepler & K. H. Rubin (Eds.), *The development and treatment of childhood aggression* (201–216). Hillsdale, NJ: Erlbaum.

Drake, J. (2003). Teacher preparation and practices regarding school bullying. *Journal of School Health,* 347–356.

Due, P., Holstein, B.E., Lynch, J., Diderichsen, F., Gabhain, S.N., Scheidt, P., et al. (2005). Bullying and symptoms among school-aged children: International comparative cross-sectional study in 28 countries. *European Journal of Public Health, 15,* 128–132.

Farrington, D. (1993). Understanding and preventing bullying. In M. Tonry (Ed.), *Crime and justice: A review of research* (Vol. 17, 381–458). Chicago: University of Chicago Press.

Fekkes, M., Pijpers, F.I.M., & Verloove-Vanhorick, S.P. (2004). Bullying behavior and associations with psychosomatic complaints in victims. *Journal of Pediatrics, 144,* 17–22.

Feldlaufer, H., Midgley, C., & Eccles, J.S. (1988). Student, teacher, and observer perceptions of the classroom environment before and after the transition to junior high school. *Journal of Early Adolescence, 8,* 133–156.

Fister, S. L. (1994). *Meeting the behavioral needs of students: A guide for administrators and program planners*. Des Moines, IA: Mountain Plains Regional Resource Center.

Foltz-Gray, D. (1996). The bully trap: Young tormentors and their victims find ways out of anger and isolation. *Teaching Tolerance, 5,* 18–23.

Forero, R., McLellan, L., Rissel, C., & Bauman, A. (1999). Bullying behavior and psychosocial health among school students in New South Wales, Australia: Cross-sectional survey. *British Medical Journal, 319,* 344–348.

Galen, B.R., & Underwood, M.K. (1997). A developmental investigation of social aggression among children. *Developmental Psychology, 33,* 589–600.

Gilmartin, B.G. (1987). Peer group antecedents of severe love-shyness in males. *Journal of Personality, 55*(3), 467–488.

Glew, G.M., Fan, M., Katon, W., Rivara, F.P., & Kernic, M.A. (2005). Bullying, psychosocial adjustment, and academic performance in elementary school. *Archives of Pediatric & Adolescent Medicine, 159,* 1026–1031.

Hall, R. V., & Hall, M. C. (1980). *How to select reinforcers.* Lawrence, KS: H & H Enterprises.

Hamre, B. K., & Pianta, R. C. (2001). Early teacher-child relationships and the trajectory of children's school outcomes through eighth grade. *Child Development, 72,* 625–638.

Hawker, D.S.J., & Boulton, M.J. (2000). Twenty years' research on peer victimization and psychosocial maladjustment: A meta-analytic review of cross-sectional studies. *Journal of Child Psychology and Psychiatry and Allied Disciplines, 41,* 441–455.

Haynie, D.L., Nansel, T., & Eitel, P. (2001). Bullies, victims, and bully/victims: Distinct groups of at-risk youth. *Journal of Early Adolescence, 21,* 29–49.

Heinemann, P.P. (1973). *Mobbning: Gruppvald blant barn og vokane* (Bullying: Group violence among children and adults). Stockholm: Natur och Kultur.

Jantzer, A.M., Hoover, J. H., & Narloch, R. (2006). The relationship between school-aged bullying and trust, shyness, and quality of friendships in young adulthood: A preliminary research note. *School Psychology International, 27,* 146–156.

Johnson, B. (2008). Teacher-student relationships which promote resilience at school: A micro-level analysis of students' views. *British Journal of Guidance & Counselling, 36*(4), 385–398.

Kaltiala-Heino, R., Rimpelae, M., Martunnen, M., Rimpelae, A., & Rantanen, P. (1999). Bullying, depression, and suicidal ideation in Finnish adolescents: School survey. *British Medical Journal, 319,* 348–351.

Kaltiala-Heino, R., Rimpelae, M., Rantanen, P., & Rimpelae, A. (2000). Bullying at school: An indicator of adolescents at risk for mental disorders. *Journal of Adolescence, 23,* 661–674.

Kärnä, A., Voeten, M., Poskiparta, E., & Salmivalli C. (2010). Vulnerable children in varying classroom contexts: Bystanders' behaviors moderate the effects of risk factors on victimization. *Merrill-Palmer Quarterly, 56,* 261–282.

Kim, Y.S., Koh, Y., & Leventhal, B. (2005). School bullying and suicidal risk in Korean middle school students. *Pediatrics, 115,* 357–363.

Klem, A. M., & Connell, J. P. (2004). Relationships matter: Linking teacher support to student engagement and achievement. *Journal of School Health, 74*(7), 262–273.

Kochenderfer-Ladd, B., & Pelletier, M.E. (2008). Teachers' views and beliefs about bullying: Influences on classroom management strategies and students' coping with peer victimization. *Journal of School Psychology, 46,* 431–453.

Kumpulainen, K., Rasanen, E., & Puura, K. (2001). Psychiatric disorders and the use of mental health services among children involved in bullying. *Aggressive Behavior, 27,* 102–110.

Limber, S.P. (2002). *Addressing youth bullying behaviors.* Proceedings from the American Medical Association Educational Forum on Adolescent Health: Youth Bullying. Chicago: American Medical Association.

Limber, S.P. (in press). Implementation of the Olweus Bullying Prevention Program: Lessons learned from the field. In D. Espelage and S. Swearer (Eds.), *Bullying in American schools: A social-ecological perspective on prevention and intervention.* Mahwah, NJ: Lawrence Erlbaum.

Limber, S.P. (in press). School and community efforts to reduce and prevent bullying. *Journal of Health Education.*

Limber, S. P. (2004). What works—and doesn't work—in bullying prevention and intervention. *Student Assistance Journal, 4,* 16–19.

Luther, S., & Zelazo, B. (2003). Resilience and vulnerability: An integrative review. In S. Luther (Ed.), *Resilience and vulnerability: Adaptation in the context of childhood adversities* (510–550). Cambridge: Cambridge University Press.

McNamara, B., & McNamara, F. (1997). *Keys to dealing with bullies.* Hauppauge, NY: Barron's.

Melton, G.B., Limber, S.P., Cunningham, P., Osgood, D.W., Chambers J., Flerx, V., Henggeler S., & Nation, M. (1998). *Violence among Rural Youth.* Final Report to the Office of Juvenile Justice and Deliquency Prevention.

Midgley, C., Feldlaughfer, H., & Eccles, J.S. (1989). Student/teacher relations and attitudes toward mathematics before and after the transition to junior high school. *Child Development, 60,* 981–992.

Mulvey, E. P., & Cauffman, E. (2001). The inherent limits of predicting school violence. *American Psychologist, 56,* 797–802.

Murray, C., & Greenberg, M.T. (2001). Relationships with teachers and bonds with school: Social emotional adjustment correlates for children with and without disabilities. *Psychology in the Schools, 38,* 25–41.

Nansel, T., Overpeck, M., Pilla, R., Ruan, W., Simons-Morton, B., & Scheidt, P. (2001). Bullying behaviors among US youth: Prevalence and association with psychosocial adjustment. *Journal of the American Medical Association, 285,* 2094–2100.

Oh, I., & Hazler, R.J. (2009). Contributions of personal and situational factors to bystanders' reactions to school bullying. *School Psychology International, 30,* 291–310.

Oliver, R., Hoover, J.H., & Hazler, R. (1994). The perceived roles of bullying in small-town midwestern schools. *Journal of Counseling and Development, 72*(4), 416–419.

Olweus, D. (1978). *Aggression in the schools: Bullies and whipping boys.* Washington, DC: Hemisphere Press (Wiley).

Olweus, D. (1991). Bully/victim problems among schoolchildren: Basic facts and effects of a school-based intervention program. In D. Pepler & K. Rubin (Eds.), *The development and treatment of childhood aggression* (411–448). Hillsdale, NJ: Erlbaum.

Olweus, D. (1993). *Bullying at school: What we know and what we can do.* Cambridge, MA: Blackwell Publishers, Inc.

Olweus, D. (1995). Bullying or peer abuse at school: Facts and intervention. *Current Directions in Psychological Science, 4*(6), 196–201.

Olweus, D. (1997). Bully/victim problems in school: Facts and intervention. *European Journal of Psychology of Education, 12*(4), 495–510.

Olweus, D. (1999). Sweden. In P.K. Smith, Y. Morita, J. Junger-Tas, D. Olweus, R. Catalano, & P. Slee (Eds.), *The nature of school bullying: A cross-national perspective* (7–27). New York: Routledge.

Olweus, D., & Limber, S. (October 20, 2010). Bullying in the U.S.: Are we making the grade? [Webinar]. Retrieved October 26, 2010, from hazelden.webex .com/ec0605lb/eventcenter/recording/recordAction.do;jsessionid=4JGZMG VWpD9P02ZGTnTnYrYvXyV2dxvh0BJTkP9Pz2BKJrfps23n!1895242519? theAction=poprecord&actname=/eventcenter/frame/g.do&apiname=lsr .php&renewticket=0&renewticket=0&actappname=ec0605lb&entappname =url0107lb&needFilter=false&&isurlact=true&entactname=/nbrRecording URL.do&rID=7094697&rKey=a21da05bf0814860&recordID=7094697&rnd =7379928472&siteurl=hazelden&SP=EC&AT=pb&format=short

O'Moore, M., & Kirkham, C. (2001). Self-esteem and its relationship to bullying behavior. *Aggressive Behavior, 27,* 269–283.

Perren, S., & Alsaker, F.D. (2006). Social behavior and peer relationships of victims, bully/victims, and bullies in kindergarten. *Journal of Child Psychology and Psychiatry, 47*(1), 45–57.

Pianta, R.C. (1994). Patterns of relationships between children and kindergarten teachers. *Journal of School Psychology, 32,* 15–31.

Pianta, R.C., Steinberg, M.S., & Rollins, K.B. (1995). The first two years of school: Teacher-child relationships and deflections in children's classroom adjustment. *Development and Psychopathology, 7,* 295–312.

Pikas, A. (1989). A pure conception of mobbing gives the best results for treatment. *School Psychology International, 10,* 95–104.

Rhode, G., Jenson, W. R., & Reavis, H. K. (1992). *The tough kid book.* Longmont, CO: Sopris West.

Rigby, K. (2002). *New perspectives on bullying.* London & Philadelphia: Jessica Kingsley.

Rivers, I., Poteat, V.P., Noret, N., & Ashurst, N. (2009). Observing bullying at school: The mental health implications of witness status. *School Psychology Quarterly, 24*(4), 211–223.

Rivers, I., & Smith, P.K. (1994). Types of bullying behaviour and their correlates. *Aggressive Behavior, 20,* 359–368.

Roberts, W. (2000). The bully as victim: Understanding bully behaviors to increase the effectiveness of interventions in the bully-victim dyad. *Professional School Counseling, 4*(2), 148–154.

Roberts, W.B. Jr., & Coursol, D.H. (1996). Strategies for intervention with childhood and adolescent victims of bullying, teasing, and intimidation in school settings. *Elementary School Guidance and Counseling, 30,* 204–213.

Roland, E., & Galloway, D. (2002). Classroom influences on bullying. *Educational Research, 44*(3), 299–312.

Salmon, G., James, A., Cassidy, E.L., & Javaloyes, M.A. (2000). Bullying a review: Presentations to an adolescent psychiatric service and within a school for emotionally and behaviourally disturbed children. *Clinical Child Psychology and Psychiatry, 5*(4), 563–579.

Schwartz, D., Gorman, A., Nakamoto, J., & Tobin, R. (2005). Victimization in the peer group and children's academic functioning. *Journal of Educational Psychology, 97,* 425– 435.

Sharp, S. (1994). How much does bullying hurt? The effects of bullying on the personal wellbeing and educational progress of secondary aged students. *Educational and Child Psychology, 12*(2), 81–88.

Shepherd, J.P., Sutherland, I., & Newcombe, R.G. (2006). Relations between alcohol, violence and victimization in adolescence. *Journal of Adolescence, 29,* 539–553.

Skinner, E.A., & Belmont, M.J. (1993). Motivation in the classroom: Reciprocal effects of teacher behavior and student engagement across the school year. *Journal of Educational Psychology, 85,* 571–581.

Smith, P.K., & Sharp, S. (Eds.). (1994). *School bullying: Insights and perspectives.* London: Routledge.

Smith, P. K., & Thompson, D. (1991). *Practical approaches to bullying.* London: David Fulton.

Smokowski, P.R., & Kopasz, K.H. (2005). Bullying in school: An overview of types, effects, family characteristics, and intervention strategies. *Children & Schools, 27*(2), 101–110.

Sourander, A., Elonheimo, H., Niemela, S., Nuutila, A. M., Helenius, H., Sillan-maki, L., et al. (2006). Childhood predictors of male criminality: A prospective population-based follow-up study from age eight to late adolescence. *Journal of the American Academy of Child and Adolescent Psychiatry, 45,* 578–586.

Sourander, A., Helstela, L., Helenius, H., & Piha, J. (2000). Persistence of bullying from childhood to adolescence—a longitudinal 8-year follow-up study. *Child Abuse & Neglect, 24,* 873–881.

Srabstein, J.C., McCarter, R.J., Shao, C., & Huang, Z.J. (2006). Morbidities associated with bullying behaviors in adolescents: School based study of American adolescents. *International Journal of Adolescent Medicine and Health, 18,* 587–596.

Swahn, M.H., Bossarte, R.M., & Sullivent, E. (2008). Age of alcohol use initiation, suicide behavior, and peer and dating violence victimization and perpetration among high-risk, seventh-grade adolescents. *Pediatrics, 121,* 297–305.

Swearer, S.M., & Doll, B. (2001). Bullying in schools: An ecological framework. *Journal of Emotional Abuse, 2,* 7–23.

Troy, M., & Stroufe, L. A. (1987). Victimization among preschoolers: Role of attachment relationship history. *Journal of the American Academy of Child and Adolescent Psychiatry, 26,* 166–172.

U.S. Census Bureau, Statistical Abstract of the United States: 2010 (129th Ed.). (2009). Washington, DC.

Van der Wal, M.F., De Wit, C.A., & Hirasing, R.A. (2003). Psychosocial health among young victims and offenders of direct and indirect bullying. *Pediatrics, 111*(6), 1312–1317.

Werner, E.E. (1990). Protective factors and individual resilience. In S.J. Meisels & J.P. Shonkoff (Eds.), *Handbook of early childhood intervention* (97–116). Cambridge: Cambridge University Press.

Werner, E.E., & Smith, R.S. (1989). *Vulnerable but invincible: A longitudinal study of resilient children and youth.* New York: Adams, Bannister & Cox.

Whitney, I., & Smith, P.K. (1993). A survey of the nature and extent of bullying in junior/middle and secondary schools. *Educational Research, 35,* 3–25.

Wolke, D., Woods, S., Bloomfield, L., & Karstadt, L. (2000). The association between direct and relational bullying and behaviour problems among primary school children. *Journal of Child Psychology and Psychiatry, 41*(8), 989–1002.

Wolke, D., Woods, S., Stanford, K., & Schulz, H. (2001). Bullying and victimization of primary school children in England and Germany: Prevalence and school factors. *British Journal of Psychology, 92,* 673–696.

INDEX

About the Author

Dr. Cricket Meehan is the coordinator of School Mental Health Projects at Miami University's Center for School-Based Mental Health Programs. She received her Ph.D. in clinical psychology from the University of Central Florida. Her scholarly work includes 10 research articles, 2 book chapters, and numerous conference presentations throughout the United States.